Platinum Principals

Making Your School a #1 Hit

By: Dianne Reynolds and Hattie Alexander

Contents

Platinum Principals

Introduction

Platinum Principals is a guide to building an effective, comprehensive school program. The most common and sometimes problematic topics faced by school administrators are explored through the lens of two seasoned principals. It is a grassroots approach to school administration that brings meaning and application to abstract concepts using music analogies. The ideology of music as a universal language that bridges people and ideas, regardless of their background, is the book's catalyst. Our personal philosophy is that school administration should play out like the production of a well-written song. When composed with the correct lyrics, melody, and rhythm, it produces a beautiful harmony. Therefore, a playlist of proven recommendations with tips for implementation is provided. This allows the reader to select strategies from various genres to enhance their specific school program.

Although our backgrounds are eclectic, we discovered that we traveled parallel paths that would finally intersect at this juncture. We both have experiences in inner-city, rural, as well as magnet school settings. By all accounts, we were considered model principals. Our schools have been named National Blue-Ribbon Schools and each of us has received the coveted Terrel H. Bell

Award for Outstanding Leadership. However, our journey to this destination was not devoid of trials and tribulations. We also shared in common sleepless nights worrying about student achievement.

Along with the accolades, our experiences include inheriting schools that were not performing well according to state accountability standards. This is where we received on-the-job training, much of which was baptism by fire. Although there is some advantage of learning from experience, we may have been spared unnecessary anguish had we known then what we know now. This prompted us to think about our paths and what we have to offer to colleagues as experienced administrators. This book is derivative of those failures and triumphs. It is a *common-sense approach* designed to help new administrators, as well as those seeking additional support or enrichment. Each chapter or genre highlights the correlation between music and the harmony that administrators seek in their everyday practices.

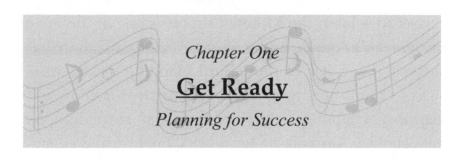

Innovative planning enables schools to prepare the 21st-century learner. Over time, the word *innovation* has become synonymous with emerging technologies. However, a more inclusive interpretation encompasses using ingenuity to solve existing problems or develop new ideas. Essentially, it is *a new way of thinking* which may include re-imagining and applying known ideas and solutions in unorthodox ways. Innovation is not limited to any subject, method, or device but is fluid in nature.

One of the best examples can be found in the establishment of the Motown Record Corporation. Berry Gordy, its founder, used the Ford Motor Company's assembly line approach of *quality control* to develop what is known as the Motown sound. This included recruiting artists, songwriters, house musicians, dance instructors, and other personnel who adhered to a set of common standards promoted by the Motown Company. Most notably, he pioneered an in-house sound and a vetting system in which personnel analyzed songs to predict their success on the charts. This innovative approach left very little to chance. It enabled his music to transcend racial boundaries and create a sound that resonated with listeners.

Decades later, the Motown sound is one of the most recognizable sounds in the world. The organization was successful because of thoughtful planning in key areas such as recruitment, culture and climate, teaching and learning, communicating, professional development, data analysis, organizing for results, finance, and engaging stakeholders. Operating from a small neighborhood home converted into an office building, Gordy proved that planning and effective resource use are more important than the resources themselves. This innovation model is applicable today for principals who are willing to re-examine their approach to school administration. Successful principals are in tune with their vision and mission. Music analogies will be used to explore some of the most prevalent education topics and issues that will assist administrators in creating a number one hit, regardless of their assignment.

There is a rare breed of people who possess innate abilities, while the rest must put forth substantial effort to be successful. The good news is that the playing field can be leveled. School administration is a career in which natural talent only goes so far. The rest is planning and laborious work. The most prolific singers have some extraordinary talent that partially explains their success. However, without committing themselves to routine application and rituals, their talent would be adversely affected.

The debut of a recording artist supports this point. This event is filled with excitement and anticipation. Backstage, the roar of the crowd reaching a crescendo can be heard before the artist takes the stage. Fans expect the delivery of a hallmark performance. This can only happen when meticulous planning has taken place to ensure a high-quality and unforgettable show. The same applies to the debut of an administrator. The school is the stage, and planning is the title of the number one hit. Professional performers prepare before their debut. It is essential to observe and critique the venue, adjust the sound system, tune-up with musicians, and have a repertoire of material to perform. Similarly, principals prepare by putting the right players in place, planning for school operations, setting the stage or environment, and preparing to meet their audience.

The Venue (Assessing the Surroundings)

Artists must assess the venue for factors such as location, desirability, capacity, parking, seating, and accessibility to restrooms, food, and drinks. The accommodation will determine if the venue is appropriate to host the concert. If the goal is to sell 40,000 tickets, then the facility and parking must accommodate that number of ticket buyers. Principals face similar tasks, including becoming familiar with the environment, staff, stakeholders, programs, and the school's financial standing. The challenge is even more significant for new principals.

Their first course of action is to get to know their surroundings, as well as understanding processes and procedures. Becoming acquainted with the office staff and reviewing newsletters of the previous principal will reveal a lot about the school. This may also include examining lesson plans to determine how instruction is approached. The school leadership team can assist by sharing information about school programs and professional development.

The next step is to meet with the bookkeeper to review the financial status of the school. Most school systems will have the books audited before a new principal assumes a position. Planning also includes talking to the custodian staff. Schedules need to be examined to determine what is necessary to do their jobs effectively. The principal should pay attention as they talk about their jobs, the good and bad. A walk around the building/grounds will help to personally identify areas in need of attention.

The next step is to delegate or access the system's method for putting in work orders to get repairs completed. Getting a handle on the building's appearance is imperative. However, "Rome was not built in a day." The goal is to clean up and repair as much as possible to make things look presentable and safe. Principals should not stress over this area as the appearance of the physical plant will take time. Making sure that it is clean and secure is more important.

Choosing the Band (Hiring Personnel)

Artists choose key players (band members) that will enhance their sound and performance. They consider their talents, style, goals, and how well they sync with others. In education, the band represents employees hired to carry out the mission and vision of the school. If the rhythm is off, it will prohibit the school from performing at its maximum potential; therefore, methodical recruitment efforts will pay great dividends. Just as candidates may request an interview, principals may seek out candidates with known skill sets that will be an asset to the school.

Creating a pool of viable candidates and closely reviewing resumes will be a time-saving measure. It is prudent to always check the candidate's references or last job. This includes new teachers and those who have just completed a college program. It is surprising how much this will help moving forward. Some candidates interview well but have poor work habits, i.e., the candidate interviewed and the one who shows up to work may appear to be two different people.

Failure to include references, although optional, may be an indication of something deeper. Also, the work history is a good source of information. It tells about the candidate's experiences and also reveals their level of commitment to their careers. Frequent lateral moves from school to school is not a good sign. If a resume leaves more questions than answers, it is a red flag. During the interview, the principal should ask open-ended questions such as the following:

1. Tell me about your background.
2. What does a typical reading or math lesson look like?

3. How do you use data to influence your instruction?

4. On a scale of 1-10, how would you rate yourself with classroom management and why?

5. What reading or math programs have you experienced using?

6. Describe how you would use technology in the classroom.

7. Explain how you meet timelines and due dates.

8. Describe how you demonstrate being a team player.

9. How do you ensure real life application of science and social studies standards?

This line of questioning requires the candidate to speak freely, divulging more information of experiences, skills, and personal philosophy. The goal is never one of embarrassment but to attain pertinent information. The principal may ask probing questions providing key clues if needed. Personal questions such as religion, age, sexual orientation, marital/family status, disability, etc. are illegal and should be avoided at all costs. There are several alerts to look for during interviews, such as inability to express ideas, lack of program knowledge, falsifying information on resumes, and lack of professionalism such as speaking negatively of another principal, employees, students, etc.

Interviews can be conducted in various ways. Some administrators interview one on one, while others prefer to interview with a team. The administrative team, department heads, or grade level leaders would be a good source of assistance for conducting interviews. Various forms can be used during the interview process, which will provide a document to refer to once the decision-making process begins. Interview forms specific to all employment areas (counselors, media specialists, coaches, paraprofessionals, registrars, bookkeepers, plant engineers, custodians, child nutrition workers, etc.) will better identify specific job-related qualifications.

Tuning Up the Instruments (School Documents)

Tuning up equipment ensures that it is ready and functioning properly when it is show time. The principal conducts a tune-up by preparing equipment and guidelines for effective operation of the school. Equipment for opening schools includes the preparation of a registration plan, handbooks, calendars, and rosters. A registration plan ensures that as many students as possible are registered before the beginning of school. Dedicating several days and teams to this endeavor prevents a rush on the first day of school. Although this will take some effort, it is a worthy investment. Compensatory time may be exchanged for teachers who volunteer. Some schools register students by last name to make the process run smoother.

Developing class rolls and/or master schedules is the second part of tuning up. Using the data card system is the most popular method used in elementary schools. Teachers complete class placement cards at the end of the previous year, identifying students by gender, ability level, behavior, and special needs. They work collaboratively to divide the students' cards up equally. However, a key factor is becoming familiar with the students to ensure a good placement decision. Ultimately, the principal is responsible for assigning the teacher's name to the roll. Counselors and curriculum specialists may assist since they are familiar with the student body. Some principals give teachers the autonomy to develop class rolls.

It must be noted that there are drawbacks to this method because it sometimes results in a conflict of interest when the distribution of power among grade levels is unequal. Therefore, students may not be equitably assigned, resulting in a disproportionate number of students with learning issues and/or behavior issues in the same class. Unfortunately, there are times they are placed with teachers who are new to the school. Ultimately, this is not good for students, teachers, or the school. The novice teacher is not likely to speak up for fear of reprisal. When assigning students to classes, it is prudent to consider variables such as personality. In rare cases, some students and teachers would not make a good match. Similarly, some parents and teachers would not pair well. Principals have the luxury of knowing this, which enables a more informed decision.

One of the most important elements of preparation is handbooks. The development of handbooks for the new year begins at the end of the previous year. It is led by the principal. During the last quarter of the year, a faculty meeting may be used for teachers to review parts of the handbook for students and parents to update and revise policies, talk about things that did not work, and make improvements. Handbooks are the principal's friend; however, staff must know what is in them to avoid making them an enemy. On too many occasions, parents violate the procedures of the school because of personnel's lack of familiarity with the handbook. This is also true when there are no procedures established at all.

Explicitly written handbooks will help the school avoid this pitfall by addressing an array of topics including school board policy and school procedures such as the school-wide discipline plan, grading policies, uniforms, arrival and dismissal, and conferences to name a few. Schools need to have sound reasoning for each procedure. It is even better when decisions are grounded in research. If this is not possible, principals must remember that *decisions made must be applied fairly to all parties; therefore, if a request cannot be duplicated for all, it should not be done for any.* For example, if some students are allowed on campus early because the parent must go to work, then all students should be allowed on campus. When in doubt, *school law 101 can be referenced—anything deemed disruptive to the school process can be prohibited.* Parents are less likely to challenge procedures that are not arbitrary. When they do, the handbook will serve as documentation.

Faculty-staff handbooks, like parent-student handbooks, outline school procedures and reiterate board policy. A copy of the handbook may be used as a working document during the year. As issues arise, they should be added and highlighted for the next year. Changes are best made when items are fresh on the principal's mind.

Matters such as attendance, dress code, duties, discipline protocol, parent communications, classroom instruction, safety, school initiatives, assessments, etc., must be addressed.

During pre-service training, staff may work in groups to present various sections of the handbook. This can serve as checking for understanding of policies and procedures. Also, engaging teachers in handbook scenarios will allow them to apply their knowledge. Employees are encouraged to frequently refer to the handbook until it becomes a habit. This can be reinforced by emailing excerpts throughout the year. Policies and procedures should be reinforced systematically and fairly. In addition to handbooks, faculty-staff calendars are a good tool to help teachers stay on schedule with events and activities of the school. The calendar should include a host of events, including professional development, data meetings, assessments, safety drills, grade level performances, student programs, etc. A calendar can be added to the Parent-Student Handbook to help parents plan for attending school-related events and reduce repeated inquiries. All dates should be considered tentative in case changes are needed.

In addition to handbooks and calendars, a form should be devised to allow teachers to sign-up for committees and duties. This is usually based on talents and interests. However, the principal may assign teachers to committees based on needs. Morning and afternoon duties should be assigned, as well. Although some principals allow teachers to select their duties, the administrative staff should be responsible for designating the areas that need to be supervised.

Arranging the Dressing Room (The Environment)

The dressing room plays a unique role in the lives of celebrities as it relates to aesthetics and accommodations. It is common to have a dressing room rider in contracts for favorite foods and beverages, while others are much more demanding such as requesting a particular variety of flowers or personal furniture shipped and arranged inside. It is unknown if the rituals are linked to a superstition that is thought to affect performance or simply a display of prima-donna behavior. Whatever the reason, there is little doubt that the demands set the tone for the performance, just as the school environment sets the tone for the year.

Principals are responsible for promoting three types of environments in the school: *physical, social,* and *emotional.* Arguably, the *physical environment* is most familiar to educators. However, the *social* and *emotional* environments are equally important. The social environment includes providing opportunities for students to engage in interest-based activities and focuses on preventative measures such as character education. The emotional environment is crucial to students' well-being and includes systems to address self-esteem, behavior, and mental health. The social and emotional environment will be discussed in subsequent chapters.

The *physical environment* of the school should be

dressed for success, considering *perception is three-fourths reality*. A parent or visitor may never speak to anyone in the school. Still, they will observe their surroundings and make assumptions. The facility should be clean and inviting with show-stopping bulletin boards. The premise is, if no one wants to stop and observe, it is futile for teachers to complete the bulletin boards. Three-dimensional thematic boards make a statement; however, criteria will need to be created to ensure all boards meet the same high standard. This may require professional development to assist teachers.

Since writing lends itself to many subjects, school-wide boards with a writing theme such as careers or favorite book (or grade level book series) are always suitable. The school environment also includes attractive data displays that convey pertinent information for stakeholders such as the following:

- a school-wide attendance display which shows classroom performance for each month
- a recreational reading board that identifies attainment of quarterly reading goals
- an assessment display to share accountability data
- basic facts display to help monitor students' achievement of math facts
- an honor roll display to highlight the academic achievement of students in the school

A classroom checklist is also important to ensure an acceptable classroom environment. It should include items such as hall displays, word walls, reading and math centers, small group instruction areas, whole group carpet areas, classroom management systems, emergency exits maps, class and school rules, consequences, student work displays, alphabets and numerals, heading format for writing, world map, and a cycle of instruction.

Schools usually take on the vision and persona of their leaders. As principal, it is important to have a vision for the environment. Ideas can be developed by visiting other buildings, attending workshops and conferences, or using social media. Elementary schools should be child-centered, full of color and uplifting scenery. Most principals favor authentic student work posted outside of classrooms. This may include students' projects and other artifacts that are displayed in the hallways throughout the school. Focus topics should be communicated to teachers each month.

Making the Debut (Introductory Meetings)

The debut is the most anticipated part of the event. Although many people are involved in the process, the audience may evaluate the concert's success by the artist's performance alone. Therefore, the performer must be primed before taking the stage. This includes loosening the vocal cords, employing proper breathing techniques, and taking care of hair, makeup, and wardrobe. It is important to make a good first impression. Principals employ similar grooming measures before meeting their audience, not by appearance alone, but by setting up forums for communication and introductions. Creating a welcome message for the staff is the first step. Normally, teachers are welcomed back through multiple modes of communication, i.e., letter, social media, and school messenger. The preservice events, dates, times, and location for the first few days of school are explicitly stated. New principals should take some time to meet the school community, including the Parent Teacher Organization (PTO). This can be done in a relaxed and informal setting such as *Donuts and Coffee with the Principal.* The administrative team should attend the event to show a united front.

Every school has customs and traditions that create lasting memories. The first day back for teachers and staff is one of those customs. Each year should begin with a celebration of the last. Theme parties such as the following create enthusiasm and serve as a mantra to motivate teachers: *Transformers* (Transforming Student Achievement), *Western* (Partners in Education), *Patriotism* (Education: The American Dream), *Sailing* (Cruising for Success), *Construction* (Building Student Achievement), *Disco* (Getting into the Groove of Learning), *Superheroes* (Education: The Superpower), or *Pirates* (Treasuring Student Success). The thematic celebrations may vary; however, one example is to host a staff breakfast that includes paraphernalia, music, and concludes with team-building games. Efforts put forth will set the tone for the new year.

A significant portion of the day is utilized to emphasize the school's vision and mission by reviewing the data from the previous year, followed by a book study related to the pertinent needs of the school. Literature is a phenomenal way to broach many subjects. Often, schools must respond to district mandates before opening; however, this activity has a far-reaching impact as it relates to promoting student achievement and a positive culture and climate.

The opening preservice needs to include new curriculum updates, in-service on new initiatives, or follow-up for existing initiatives, data review, and curriculum strategies to ensure effective implementation of programs. At this time, teachers should be given the tools needed to start the year. Items should be organized by grade level for distribution. They include lesson plan binders, gradebooks, attendance binders, schedule booklets, curriculum grade level pacing guides, handbooks, communication folders for students, school-specific initiatives, materials, and classroom rolls.

After teachers have been given the necessary information, they need time to meet in their respective grade levels to bond and plan for instruction. Providing a grade-level mentor for new teachers will ensure they are acclimated to expectations. The process includes reviewing the standards, new textbooks, and online programs. The development of collaborative lesson plans, strategies, and materials should also be discussed. Grade-level collaborations build continuity. The first week of curriculum planning should include rules and procedures of the school, as well as the classroom.

Although most schools host a meet and greet before school, not all students and parents will attend. Therefore, the principal will still need to introduce herself to the student body. Every effort should be made to visit each classroom during the first week. With the opening of school responsibilities, this may be difficult. In lieu of in-class introductions, an assembly may be held or the introduction may be videotaped by the broadcasting club, followed by a quick tour of each classroom. After the introduction to students, the next step is a formal introduction to parents. Although most open houses closely follow the opening of school, parents will want to hear from the principal once the school opens. A welcome back parent newsletter covering housekeeping items such as arrival and dismissal, procedures, parent meetings, and pertinent dates can be sent home on the first day of school.

How the school begins the year will largely determine the type of year it will experience; therefore, preparation for opening is key. There are many responsibilities that must be taken care of before the opening of school. The following is a list of items that will need to be completed:

To-Do List

- o Interviews
- o Meetings (Bookkeeper, Leadership, Staff, PTO)
- o Class Rolls
- o Registration Team
- o Schedules (Masters, Teachers, Custodians, Support Personnel)
- o Handbooks (Faculty-Staff, Parent- Student)
- o Faculty-Staff Roster

o Calendars (Faculty-Staff, Parent-Student)
o Duty Rosters (Morning, Afternoon, Late Pick Up)
o Late pick-up letter
o Bulletin Boards Themes
o Discipline Referral Forms (Classroom, Administrative)
o Parent Communication Folders
o Transportation Labels
o Student Transportation Forms
o Dismissal Logs
o Assessment Calendar
o Committees List
o Student Demographic Form
o Behavior Folder
o Lesson Plans
o Back to School Celebration for Staff
o First day of school plan (duty, registration team/procedures/assignments, etc.)
o Substitute Schedule (data meetings)
o Classroom Intercom List
o Emergency Drills
o Open House Activities

Chapter Two

The Way You Do the Things You Do!

Culture and Climate

School culture is defined as the shared beliefs of the school organization, while *school climate* refers to the impact the culture has on students and stakeholders. Culture and climate are like the rhythm of a song. The Greek word *rhythmos* is derived from *rhein* which means "to flow." School cultures have a repetitive and unique way in which they operate or flow. The climate is established when stakeholders systematically respond to the rhythm or culture of the school. This can be a positive toe-tapping experience or one symbolized by folded arms in which stakeholders choose to sit out. Culture and climate are impacted by every aspect of the school program; however, it is the interactions and beliefs of its stakeholders that are most significant.

This can be most clearly seen within the principal's leadership and interactions with students, employees, and parents. A positive culture and climate maintain the steady beat of the school program.

Going Platinum (Elements of a Platinum Principal)

Research identifies the principal as one of the most important influences on student achievement, as well as culture and climate. They are referred to here as *Platinum* principals. In the music industry, platinum means an album has been widely successful, sold one million copies, and has a single that has sold two million. In education, *a platinum principal possesses the right elements to build a sound program that results in a high level of student achievement, balanced by stakeholder satisfaction.*

Platinum is an element that consists of rare precious metal. It is characterized by its *dense, malleable, ductile,* and *high melting* point attributes. A *dense* or concentrated quality allows the principal to be grounded in research-based best practices that have been authenticated and extrapolated across subject matter and time. At the core are reading and math programs that promote critical thinking and problem solving, student engagement, inquiry, and an infusion of technology.

The *malleable* and *ductile* traits give the principal the flexibility to extensively stretch and bend without breaking. This soft skill is valuable when addressing unforeseen daily issues and collaborating with stakeholders. Situations such as buses arriving late, unplanned interruptions, or numerous teachers absent on the same day require an immediate response from the principal. It is the same trait that allows flexibility when compromising with teachers on instructional practices, lesson plans, and other meaningful issues.

The *high melting point* makes the platinum principal resilient and composed in heated situations, which enables rational decision-making. This includes high-stress situations such as responding to medical emergencies of students and staff, missing students, angry parents, or safety emergencies.

Platinum principals, like musicians, conduct frequent sound checks to determine the quality of their school's performance. All systems must be synchronized to keep the audience engaged. Sound checks must be conducted before the concert begins and again during intermission. This ensures all parts of the program are working as designed. Principals must constantly gauge and monitor the practices of the school, as well as public opinions of those practices through interactions with students, employees, parents, and visitors.

Soundcheck #1(Students)

Sound check #1 focuses on students and character education which is the foundation for developing a healthy *social environment.* The goal of education is to produce productive members of society. Good students should become better through school experiences. Activities such as the *CD of the Day* (Character Demonstrator of the Day) make this a reality. The CD of the Day involves each teacher selecting a student who has displayed one of the six pillars of character and a brief description of the act. The form is sent to the counselor before the end of the day. The counselor then reads each submission and selects one student as CD of the Day. The student's name and pillar of character is written on a CD and displayed on the school-wide CD board.

Activities such as a weekly *character assembly* go beyond teaching the pillars of character by addressing citizenship, bullying, the moral of the story, sportsmanship, etc. It is implemented by collaborating with the school counselor, media specialist, technology teacher, and physical education teacher. During assemblies, teachers present activities by grade levels within their respective areas. The counselor presents activities related to character development and patriotism including learning the history of patriotic symbols and singing patriotic songs. The media specialist uses literature to teach the moral of the story while addressing other prevalent issues. The physical education teacher reinforces concepts such as sportsmanship and movement. The technology teacher works with colleagues to integrate a technology component to presentations. Character assemblies serve a dual purpose: to promote character and attendance while providing supervision of students as teachers attend weekly professional development.

The assemblies also help to reinforce and monitor daily attendance and behavior. Students wear two-sided point cards to encourage attendance and positive behavior. A tardy song is played each morning to encourage timely arrival. A point is received for arriving to class before the tardy song ends. The song is motivational in nature to get students ready for the day. Parents can hear the song as they drive up, which encourages them to move expeditiously, as well. Students also receive a daily point for positive behavior. The point cards are marked for 20 days. At the end of the 20-day period, the counselor creates a PowerPoint presentation to share each class's performance (behavior and attendance) during the assembly. This holds students accountable for their actions.

Other activities that support character education include identifying students to include on the counselor watch list—*C.A.R.S.* (Counseling Assistance and Routine Support) and the *Second Chance Program. C.A.R.S.* is a morning check-in system in which the counselor conducts classroom visits to personally speak with students who need extra support. This provides an opportunity to review expectations before beginning their day. The *Second Chance Program* is an afterschool program for students who have displayed behaviors that violate the school's code of conduct. The program significantly reduces the number of out-of-school suspensions and allows prevailing issues to be addressed through small group counseling. Students are also assigned a mentor as needed. Although the counselor is instrumental in promoting character education, classroom teachers must also support students by creating a positive environment and *building* on the following concepts:

Bonding and establishing relationships.
Understanding there may be underlying issues.
Identifying students' passions and using it for instruction.
Listening and observing.
Developing self-regulating strategies, consequences, and rewards.

Just as positive actions affect students' behavior, so do negative actions. Some students are susceptible to aggressive responses that tend to exacerbate inappropriate behavior. The following *triggers* escalate the very behaviors that schools seek to eliminate:

- Yelling or making physical contact
- Embarrassing students in front of peers
- Making verbal threats which causes panic and anxiety
- Invading students' personal spaces, causing a fight or flight response
- Making derogatory statements that affect self-esteem
- Bickering with students which places the teacher at the child's level
- Marking and tearing up students' work, making them feel de-valued
- Taking and trashing personal items which may be the child's only possession
- Allowing bullying to go unaddressed, leaving students to fend for themselves
- Failing to prepare for instruction creating a poor classroom environment
- Leaving students unattended causing an unsafe environment
- Instituting practices and bias treatments that give some students an unfair advantage over others

Building character includes understanding diversity, which should be an interdisciplinary part of students' course of study. It may be accomplished through classroom practices but also through related literature. Doing so provides an opportunity for real-world application of social skills and has the added benefit of reinforcing comprehension skills such as the main idea, understanding characters, inferencing, author's purpose, citing text evidence, and text-to-self and text-to-world connections. Diversity awareness not only combats normalizing prejudices related to race or ethnic background but socioeconomic status, physical appearance, gender, age, religion, etc. Students are not born prejudice. Instead, it is developed and perfected over time through observations and interactions. When schools fail to intervene, they consent through silence. Often prejudice and cliquish behavior are viewed as preference. This is evident on the elementary playground when a student is ostracized by other students and overlooked as child's play.

Teachers should not ignore or accept this behavior but instead use it as a teachable moment. Activities such as using a *Buddy Bag* allow students to pull a classmate's name out of a bag to interact with during recess or free play at least once per week. They then share one positive thing they learned about their classmate with the class. This activity urges them to get to know students who may be of a different race, culture, etc. A positive *social environment* also demonstrates a balance and appreciation of talents and interests of all students by going beyond reading and math to be more inclusive of extra-curricular activities in which students get to express themselves through multiple mediums.

Initiatives such as the Primary Years Program (PYP),

Middle Years Program (MYP), and the Diploma Program (DP) of the International Baccalaureate Programme enrich student education and connection to others globally. The programs provide students with a framework on how to look at life from the perspectives of others and not just themselves. This initiative requires commitment from a group of stakeholders, the district, school board, teachers, and parents. It is an elementary curriculum of distinction that offers students the opportunity to take their learning to a new level. The curriculum of the PYP programs uses an interdisciplinary and inquiry-based approach that strongly supports most science and social studies curriculums, as well as state standards. Program instruction is organized around the following themes:

1. Who we are
2. How the world works
3. How we organize ourselves
4. Sharing the planet
5. Where we are in place and time
6. How do we express ourselves?

The IB program is also in alignment with the nations effort to promote STEM and interpersonal relationships through social science. Activities include hands-on science labs, school-based global tours, geography bees, Black History programs, and science night. These programs become an integral part of the overall culture of the school. Additionally, many of the educational excursions that students engage in during the school year enhances IB, science and social studies concepts. Teachers work as a collaborative team to developed thematic units of inquiry that are aligned to state standards.

What is PYP?

◆It is a transdisciplinary programme of international education designed to foster the development of the whole child.

> Transdisciplinary means pertaining to or involving more than one discipline. The Whole Child: healthy, safe, engaged, supported, challenged

◆ The IB Primary Years Programme is for students ages 3 to12 and focuses on the development of the child as an inquirer, both in the classroom and the world outside.

◆ The PYP is a framework guided by six transdisciplinary themes of global significance, explored using knowledge and skills derived from six subject areas, with a powerful emphasis on inquiry based learning.

◆ The PYP promotes the construction of knowledge by providing opportunities for children to build meaning and refine understanding, principally through structured inquiry.

◆ The PYP emphasizes meaning and understanding, and importance is attached in all areas of the curriculum--the written, the taught, and the assessed -- to the exploration of a core set of concepts.

◆ The PYP promotes international mindedness.

◆ The PYP requires valid and varied assessment.

The PYP program is made up of the written curriculum, taught curriculum, and learned curriculum. Students engage in a school-wide focus on character education that underlines the learner's profile. The written curriculum is developed by the teachers in the PYP school. The focus is what do we want the students to learn:

- *Form.* What is it like?
- *Function.* How does it work?
- *Causations.* Why is it like it is?
- *Change.* How is it changing?
- *Connection.* How is it connected to other things?
- *Perspective.* What are the points of view?
- *Responsibilities.* What is our responsibility?

PYP units are correlated, and teachers use the state standards to make sure students matriculate through the appropriate curriculum correctly. The school's curriculum or *Program of Inquiry* (POI) is displayed as one walks into any PYP school throughout the world. Students develop projects that share their findings and interest after a unit is taught. They move through 36 units during their time at a PYP school from grades K-5. The last unit is developed and executed in a setting called *Exhibition,* which is conducted by the 5th graders at the end of the school year.

Students start working on this endeavor at the beginning of their 5th-grade year. This involves them doing research on their topics. The media specialist and teachers teach students the correct way to use the research (MLA method) and how to cite and extract information from websites, articles, and books. They receive and understand the honesty policy that is developed for the school by the staff. Students work in teams to organize the information and finally present it to the community and parents. They organize charity events, donate money, volunteer time to organizations, help other people and animals, or find ways to improve the environment. They get the other students in the school involved in their philanthropy. Students in the PYP only have the framework for the International Baccalaureate (IB) Program. Still, it helps them as they move on to the MYP and DP programs. Most of all, the PYP programs provide students at an early age with social, communication, thinking, research, and self-management skills. It also teaches them to think and act locally, as well as globally.

Soundcheck #2 (Employees)

Soundcheck #2 explores the employee's role in culture and climate. Maintaining a positive culture and climate can sometimes become more important than what students are learning. In a healthy culture, the principal delegates authority and collaborates with the building leadership team, grade-level chairpersons, lead teachers, reading and math coaches, teams, and others to deliver an effective program. They are also responsible for helping staff to sustain the mental challenges of the job. A staff that is not inspired will not perform at their optimal level. Factors such as *change* and *morale* significantly impact teachers' abilities to perform their jobs. Each must be targeted and strategically addressed. Change is often the most difficult, as most people are creatures of habit.

Once there is a familiarity with a process or program, there is a reluctance to change. This may result in *subtle sabotage* in which minimal effort is put forth to ensure success. Reservations are sometimes linked to fear or competence level, similar to that of an artist who must duplicate success following a hit record. The fear may be that the new record will never be as good as the last; therefore, it is better not to try. The principal is instrumental in changing this outlook by providing a scaffold for employees, including open dialogue and professional development. *School changes should come in increments and never be abruptly instituted, except in cases of safety.* Introducing change in schools normally brings about resistance and an *Implementation Dip (Fullan, 2001).* That is, performance with new programs or strategies reverts all teachers to a novice level. This is most uncomfortable for veteran teachers.

As educators refine their skills, it is essential to do so in a positive school climate. Therefore, efforts must be taken to maintain staff *morale* by planning appreciation events beyond teacher appreciation week. Morale boosters include activities such as achievement certificates or honor roll for teachers, quarterly team celebrations, duty-free lunch or teacher recess, *Kudos Cards* for good Samaritan acts, and *comp coupons* for extended hours beyond the regular school day. Coupons are named after the school's mascot *(Beautiful Bee Award, Awesome Autobot Award, Terrific Tiger Award, Eager Eagle Award, Shining Star Award, and Rad Ram Award).* With the principal's approval, employees may use the coupons for early dismissals such as doctor's appointments or just as a simple brain break. Participation in events is significantly increased by this small token of appreciation.

Staff morale can be promoted in other ways, as well. *Off-Campus Collaboration (OCC)* allows teachers to have a working lunch (planning session) with colleagues at a local restaurant once per quarter. Minutes of the planning session should be documented and submitted upon their return. Education is one of the few professions in which employees are expected to eat lunch and supervise children simultaneously. The morale boosters provide an opportunity to collaborate as professionals. Students are the ultimate beneficiaries of a positive culture and climate.

Soundcheck #3 (Parents and Visitors)

The opinion of those outside of the school can often become the reality. Therefore, principals must continuously conduct sound checks with parents and visitors. The first perception of the school is gathered through interactions with the office staff. It is important that employees are courteous and accommodating by addressing visitors immediately. However, should principals want parents to convey an accurate interpretation of the school, it will require an additional step in which parents are educated about the school program and its goals. If not, the perception will be based on the acts of a few individuals, such as a teacher, office personnel, or the carpool line director.

The first formal meeting should include a *school focus* presentation to orient parents to the school program by reviewing expectations, providing an overview of initiatives, explaining the results of accountability and benchmark data from the previous year, and sharing goals for the upcoming year for attendance, discipline, assessments, and technology acquisition. School data should always be transparent. If it is good, parents need to celebrate the achievement. If not, they need to know how to contribute to its change. Either way, they become informed stakeholders.

If Walls Could Talk (Self-Assessment)

Although it is important for the principal to assess the culture and climate of the school, *stakeholder perception is even more important*. The perception may differ greatly based on experience. Credence to this idea can be found in the old blues song, "If Walls Could Talk." The personification suggests that walls have human-like qualities with the ability to see and hear things that do not meet the eye. Similarly, there are subliminal messages that schools may unintentionally convey to the public. To avoid this phenomenon, a self-assessment of the school's culture and climate is necessary. There are a variety of perception surveys available for areas of the school program. Schools must consider the concrete evidence to support each rating. Honesty and reflection are essential during this process. Assessing the culture and climate should begin with a self-assessment by school officials, followed by parents, students, and community stakeholders. The following areas should be examined:

Self-Assessment Questions

Student Interaction	Is character education promoted in the school? Are students treated fairly and disciplined with decorum? What student organizations does the school have, and do they have a voice in decision-making? How is student achievement celebrated? Is student achievement a priority? Do students monitor their data?
Parent Interactions	Are parents welcomed into the school? What communications methods are established? What parent activities and programs are available? How are parents allowed to share input in the school improvement process? Is student achievement a priority? Is data transparent and shared in an understandable format?

Staff Interactions	How are staff treated and supported? What decision-making power do they have? What celebrations are held? How is student achievement prioritized? How is data used to improve instruction?
Physical Environment	Is the environment clean and conveys a sense of pride and high expectations? Are there established criteria for bulletin boards? Does the school display students' work?
Professional Development	Do teachers reflect on instruction? How are professional development needs determined and delivered? Does professional development address an array of topics?
Research Based-Best Practices	What initiatives are utilized in the school? Are practices research-based? Do they address identified needs of students? Is professional development provided for proper implementation?
Technology	How is technology integrated into the curriculum? Have teachers been trained in authentic implementation? Has an acceptable use policy been developed? Does the technology plan include maintenance and updates?
Diversity	Are there images in the school that are reflective of the population served? What activities does the school implement to recognize diversity, such as multicultural studies? Are special needs students included in activities?
Creative Expression	What creative outlets are available for students? Does the school provide opportunities for students to engage in activities such as music, drama, dancing, singing, and art?
Leadership	Are teachers encouraged to be leaders? What opportunities are made available? How does the principal build leadership capacity?
Curriculum	Are reading, math, science, and social studies programs research-based? How is pacing determined? Does the curriculum address the whole child? Are learning styles considered during instruction?

Marketing	How is the school marketed to the public? Are there procedures to share events and successes of the school? How is social media utilized?
Assessments	How are formative and summative assessments used in the school? Do assessments match the intended outcome? Are they vetted for fairness and bias-free?
Safety	Does the school have a safety plan? Are safety drills uniformly practiced? Are teachers assigned to morning and afternoon duties? Do parents show proper identification for early dismissals? Do visitors report to the office before moving about the building? Are doors locked during school hours?
School Funds	What funding sources does the school have, and how are they used? Are funds aligned to maximize impact? What resources are purchased for students' use?

Culture and climate refer to *the way we do the things we do.* It is the actions and perceptions that make one school different from all others. While there are different interpretations of what this looks like in schools, there are concrete steps that uniformly lead to a positive environment that is inclusive of all stakeholders. Subsequent chapters will explore additional components of culture and climate that will greatly impact the school's success.

Chapter Three
<u>ABC</u>
Teaching and Learning

There is some debate on which elements make a hit song; however, most agree that key components include storyline, catchy tune, lyrics, and hook. The combined elements, when balanced, help to produce the most popular hits. When designing the school program, the included elements are just as important as what is excluded. Too often, administrators are inundated with what is fashionable in education; however, a good solid program is not based on what is new, instead on what works. Many programs use buzzwords from reputable sources such as National Council of Teachers of Mathematics or College and Career Ready Standards; however, the programs themselves may still have little impact on student learning.

Before selecting a program, principals should conduct research and keep in mind that just because a program claims to be researched-based does not mean it is applicable to their school. A sound reading, math, science, or social studies program *will* have some of the same components, but contrary to popular belief, all schools are not the same and may not have the same needs or deficiencies. Schools should determine students' needs by looking at trend data and then evaluating potential programs according to their success rate in addressing similar deficiencies. Teachers should vet the proposed program to ensure buy-in for implementation. Once this is done, the pieces begin to fit together. Proven methodologies are used to represent the *storyline*; daily practices represent the *catchy tune*. Curriculum and standards are followed, symbolizing the *lyrics*, and essential components of instruction are repeated across the school, constituting the *hook*.

Story Line (Pedagogy)

The *storyline* of a song provides meaning and purpose. Theory, methodology, and pedagogy have a similar function in education by serving as the framework for delivering effective instruction. Well-rounded school programs incorporate various theories of learning. Piaget's *social cognitive theory* is a reminder that instruction is time-sensitive and depends on where students are on the academic spectrum. It must be noted that this has nothing to do with age or grade level but the depth of knowledge the student has mastered. For example, students in fourth grade who have not mastered subtracting with regrouping will have difficulty with the concept of long division; therefore, the scope and sequence of instruction must be tailored to meet students at their developmental levels.

Prerequisite knowledge is necessary for students to advance through concept. There are no shortcuts. When educators ignore this fact, it forces students into an alternate reality which results in failure. Extensive intervention may be necessary to prepare students for grade-level content, which means that students may not initially perform well on grade-level assessments; however, with adequate support, the achievement gap can be closed.

If students are to become critical thinkers and problem solvers, they must construct their own meaning as suggested by Dewey's *constructivism theory*. The emergence of programs that claim to foster this type of instruction have become prevalent. With it has come the challenge to develop teachers' facilitating skills to help students integrate new knowledge into what they already know. Student-led instruction requires the teacher to become a master craftsman who is skilled at getting the desired learning outcomes. The *flipped classroom* (self-study), *cooperative learning* (group learning), and *project-based learning* (research-based learning) are all student-centered approaches in which the teacher must monitor and strategically guide students' learning. This requires extensive planning, higher-order questioning techniques, and the development of rubrics for performance levels, i.e., professional development. It is also imperative that educators remember the role of *direct instruction* to address skills that students may be lacking. Students must have a framework if they are to build their own knowledge.

Equally important to pedagogy is remembering that students have learning styles that vary. Historically, teachers have relied on the lecture method, which is geared towards the *auditory learner* who needs to hear information in order to retain it. However, this method may be made more effective by utilizing strategies such as turn and talk, cooperative learning, or engaging in a debate. Other students are *visual learners* who need to see visual representations to understand concepts. This is particularly true when teaching mathematics and science. Building conceptual understanding brings meaning and depth to students' learning. The visual learner benefits from illustrations, videos, graphic organizers, charts, graphs, etc.

Instruction for the *kinesthetic learner* need to include physical interactions. The premise is students learn by doing; therefore, the focus is on engagement. Activities include using manipulatives, role-playing, movement, etc. All learning styles may incorporate the use of technology to enhance students' understanding. This can only happen with purposeful planning in which the teacher seeks authentic learning opportunities and uses the technology to further the learning goal. The disadvantage to this method is the misconception that computers teach students. Therefore, instruction becomes more about the technology instead of the standards. Teachers must keep in mind that technology is only as effective as the instructor.

Catchy Tune (Daily Practices)

Most memorable songs generally have a *catchy tune* or a sort of familiarity. In education, this indelible tune represents regular daily practices that take place in schools. Successful schools implement an array of school-wide strategies to systematically address deficient skills and concepts based on data. Like a catchy tune, the strategies are easily adapted into the school program. The practices are systematic, impactful ways to improve students' academic achievement. They are most effective when based on longitudinal data related to school-wide deficiencies.

Daily practices such as *Say It Again Synonyms* are used to improve and accelerate students' vocabulary. It is implemented by choosing a focus or overused word for each week of the year. The goal is to use the focus word as an anchor for students to learn new words that are synonymous. For example, the word *happy* is a word that is commonly used by students, so it would be chosen as the focus word. Five additional words are selected for the week (ecstatic, euphoric, exuberant, jovial, and elated). On Monday's announcements, the principal would then say, "It's time for our Say It Again Synonym. Our focus word for this week is happy. Happy is an adjective that means feeling or showing pleasure. Teachers, please write the synonyms for happy on the board as I say them aloud: ecstatic, e-c-s-t-a-t-i-c." This is continued until all words are read and spelled. The announcement on Monday would conclude by saying, "I challenge you to use these words when you are speaking and writing this week."

Tuesday's announcement includes using the words in context. The principal proceeds as follows, "It is time for our Say It Again Synonyms. Our focus word for this week is happy. Synonyms for happy are ecstatic, euphoric, exuberant, jovial, and elated. I could say: Ms. Smith was happy that her students won the spirit trophy. Or, I could say: Ms. Smith was ecstatic that her students won the spirit trophy. Another way of saying it is: Ms. Smith was euphoric that her students won the spirit trophy. I challenge you to use these words when you are speaking and writing this week." It is a good idea to use sentences that relate to teachers, students, and events in the school to pique students' interests.

The same process used on Tuesday is used on Wednesday and Thursday. The activity for Friday includes a sentence for each word (5 total) written by students from an assigned class. A calendar for classes scheduled to complete sentences is developed at the beginning of the year. If the principal chooses, the *Say It Again Synonyms* strategy may be completed by designated students during the morning news broadcast, counselor, reading coach, or a lead teacher. The purpose of the strategy is to improve and enrich students' vocabulary. Focus words are taken from the most commonly used words in students' journal writings. It is recommended to use at least three words that will stretch students' vocabulary. Younger students may be given two to three words instead of five. Each teacher is required to keep a *Say It Again Synonym* poster of words on their door. Words are removed at the end of the grading period and replaced with new ones. Students are encouraged to use the words in their daily writing. The greatest benefit can be seen over time. As students encounter the words each year, they become a regular part of their vernacular, which is the ultimate goal.

Daily word wall activities may also be used to increase student knowledge. A number of skills can be taught, including support for spelling and writing; sight words; alphabetical order, dictionary skills; phonetic patterns;

rhyming words; beginning and ending sounds; medial sounds, synonyms, and much more. A brief daily routine includes activities such as *I'm thinking of a word* in which one student would say: I'm thinking of a word that begins like *father*, but rhymes with *sound* (found); I'm thinking of a word that begins with *a* and means the opposite of *question* (answer); or I'm thinking of a word that begins with *t* and comes after *teacher* in the dictionary (trouble). The word wall can significantly improve spelling and writing skills if made a routine part of the day.

Using bell ringers is a quick and easy way to address school-wide deficiencies. By doing so, students grasp grade-level content more easily. A daily review system such as the context clues bell ringer activity (3-5 examples) incorporates a slide presentation in which the teacher introduces and models how to use context clues to determine the meaning of the word in question. After modeling, the teacher provides guided practice for students. Eventually, students are expected to turn and talk to discuss their answers. Lastly, they match their answer to the answer choice that is most closely related. This allows processing without guessing on multiple-choice items. Students also benefit from the use of exit slips which provide an efficient way to express what they have learned and teachers to assess progress towards the learning goal.

Lyrics (State Standards)

Lyrics are the explicitly written language of a song.

The words lay the foundation expressed by the artist, just as state standards lay the foundation for instruction. In order to teach the necessary skills, teachers must unpack the state standards. This allows for an in-depth understanding of how each skill is taught. Most standards are multifaceted and require more than a cursory glance. That is, teachers must not rely on keywords but the full scope of the standard. The following example shows a reading literature standard for third and fifth grade:

> Compare and contrast the themes, settings, and plots and stories written by the same author about the same or similar characters (Alabama ELA Standard – RL3.9) and compare and contrast stories in the same genre on their approaches to similar themes and topics. (Alabama ELA Standard – RL5.9).

At first glance, the standard requires students to compare and contrast. It is *what* they are to compare and contrast that is key. Third-grade students are comparing elements of a story by the same author or same topic. In contrast, fifth-grade students must compare stories in the same genre with similar themes. The latter is more rigorous and requires a higher level of analytical skills. To ensure all standards are taught, many districts provide pacing guides that outline each grade level's scope and sequence of instruction.

Writing is also an important part of teaching standards. Beginning in kindergarten, students should develop their handwriting skills while simultaneously engaging in the writing process. While addressing foundational handwriting skills, teachers may begin instructing students to express their thoughts and ideas. Initially, much of the instruction will be verbal, in which students practice making complete sentences. The writing process for younger students might include nonconventional spellings. Nevertheless, students need to begin to see how letters become words and how ideas can be expressed in a sentence.

Teachers can scaffold instruction by helping students to clarify their thoughts and edit their work during the writing conference. For kindergarten and first grade students, this may include sentences dictated to the teacher, or it may be student-written and then *mirrored* (written correctly) by the teacher. This will depend on where the student is developmentally. Again, the goal is to move students toward understanding that language consists of sounds that are translated into letters; letters and sounds formulate words; words make sentences; and sentences/ paragraphs communicate one's thinking. By the end of the year, first-grade students should understand writing mechanics and be able to write a paragraph about their ideas.

Requirements should gradually increase as students progress from lower grades (K-2) to upper grades (3-5). Students in upper elementary should be able to write in narrative, descriptive, and explanatory modes. To do so, teachers should model and use graphic organizers so that students may organize their thoughts. Modeled samples should be displayed in the classroom for future reference. Instruction in upper elementary should also focus on cursive handwriting.

Standards that are taught should be outlined in lesson plans. This will ensure the necessary content is covered. Schools are different and require different templates for instructional plans. Collaborative lesson plans may be completed by grade levels. Teachers should meet weekly to determine the content. This will ensure that all students are getting an equitable education. It is a good idea for teachers to use an instructional format of delivery so that expectations are the same. Each subject should include materials and supplies, essential vocabulary, modeling, guided practice, independent practice, and small group instruction. The use of technology and higher-order questions should also be pre-determined.

The Hook (Instruction and Intervention)

The *hook* is an intentional phrase that captures the essence of the song. It is often confused with the song's title because of its routine repetition. Although the phrase itself may be very short and simple, it is most powerful to the overall success of the song, just as instructional hooks are imperative to the school program's success. They include systematic delivery of whole group, small group, individualized instruction and intervention. Whole group instruction is crucial, as it is the first delivery of the core program; thereby, negating the need for extensive remediation. Small group instruction follows whole group instruction and provides a deeper focus on targeted skills of the core program. It should be purposeful and calibrated throughout the school to ensure effectiveness. It needs to provide a deeper focus on the targeted skills of the core program. Teachers must know exactly what each student needs in order to decrease deficiencies.

Assuming the student has not mastered concepts from whole group, modeling is even more crucial. Too often, small group instruction begins with the teacher asking the student to perform tasks instead of using the opportunity to correctly demonstrate concepts to be mastered. This results in an ineffective use of time and minimal learning. Small group instruction should also increase student engagement and provide more authentic opportunities to read. When facing assessments, students will encounter unfamiliar text. Keeping this in mind, they need multiple opportunities to individually engage with the text before reading verbally. This allows time for processing needed to read independently.

In addition, stating a purpose for reading upfront provides meaning for students as they perform the task. *Example: The author stated that the main character was "green with envy." Read page 38 to find out why. What evidence supports the statement?* Setting a purpose increases comprehension. Providing frequent opportunities to re-read text increases comprehension, fluency, and word recognition.

Implementing small group instruction in elementary school is the final time to make sure that fundamental reading skills are in place. Fifth grade is the last year in most elementary schools. Thus, teachers need to continue to provide small group instruction as needed for these students. Sometimes schools move too quickly into departmentalizing. This typically results in a heavy emphasis on whole group instruction, which should not be the case. These students need intense instruction because they will be moving to the next level.

Small group instruction is not prevalent in most middle and high school programs; therefore, it is very important to give students this last opportunity to mature as they grow academically. Whole group and small group instruction taught to fidelity will close most achievement gaps; however, some students will still need additional support. Individualized instruction is intense remediation utilized when students do not respond to whole or small group instruction. Depending on the model used, it is delivered by a special education teacher. However, in some models, the general education teacher works with students individually.

It is important to supplement whole group and small group instruction with instructional *intervention* to close achievement gaps. Therefore, as many employees as possible should have an intervention group including general education teachers, special education teachers, instructional aides, physical education teachers, media specialists, speech teachers, bookkeepers, art teachers, music teachers, registrars, and custodians (if qualified). The selection of intervention personnel depends on the culture and climate of the school. If a strong culture and climate exist, principals will have few problems soliciting additional help from support personnel. The classroom teacher should determine what skills are reinforced during intervention through diagnostic and benchmark assessments.

An intervention kit should be created for intervention personnel. Concepts taught must be within the knowledge range of the person using it. If possible, intervention should be done at the beginning of the day so that employees may resume their regular duties. The teacher must be careful that intervention does not become a substitute for solid core instruction. When core instruction is not implemented to fidelity, the teacher may find herself constantly trying to close the achievement gap by providing remediation. Negative outcomes can quickly spiral out of control; therefore, it is imperative that the first delivery follow the cycle of instruction with a deep emphasis on checking for understanding.

Chapter Four

I Heard It Through the Grapevine

Communicating with Parents

Music is a universal language used to communicate a variety of messages. There are distinct differences in each kind. Country music songs are typically simplistic in lyrics and storytelling. Artists are very descriptive of events in the song. On the other hand, blues songs convey how characters feel instead of telling a story. The songs often describe the emotional fallout after relationships have gone bad or the euphoria experienced when they are going well. Both country and blues songs leave very little doubt of the author's purpose. However, classical music tends to be more complex. It can be extremely dramatic with high energy, yet romantic in nature, evoking images of beauty. The intricacies force the listener to infer its meaning; thus, leaving various interpretations. On the contrary, communicating with parents cannot be left to interpretation. It must be clear and succinct.

The Maestro (The Art of Communication)

Principals are the head conductors or *maestros* of communication in the school from which staff takes their cues. They must also cultivate a positive relationship with the public ensuring that interactions are *professional, prepared, and polished*. Be it daily announcements on the intercom, speaking at a school program, hosting a parent conference, or using the voice messaging system, the principal is always on stage. Therefore, each occasion must be approached *professionally*. This means operating from an ethical standpoint, following board policy, and using discretion and confidentiality in all situations.

In the age of technology, it is highly likely that anything said or done has been captured electronically. This snapshot should be the best representation of the principal instead of a caricature on a bad day. Principals must also be *prepared* by gathering the necessary information, research, or background knowledge to carry out communication tasks. Time is a premium commodity for parents and educators; therefore, preparation will make meetings more efficient and productive. If it is a parent conference about child development or a student's academic performance, the principal should know her research, and better yet, know what steps the teacher has implemented to help the student. It may also be prudent to have a plan of action prepared based on the parent's concerns. Doing so demonstrates knowledge. Lack of preparation leaves the door open for unwanted consequences.

Lastly, communication with parents requires that the principal is *polished*. This enables a smooth delivery that is easily understood. Many administrators lose credibility for failure to complete this last step. When speaking publicly, it is imperative to rehearse the delivery of information to avoid a faux pas. Principals should create a system or script for intercom announcements and voice messaging. Just as most accidents occur close to home, speaking accidents most commonly happen during routine activities such as previously mentioned. A polished delivery exudes confidence and believability. There are occasions where the principal is expected to act extemporaneously, but this should not be commonplace. What is said cannot be retrieved.

Principals are also characterized by how they project themselves non-verbally. Because they have not had the opportunity to build relationships, those who are new to the profession are sometimes scrutinized more closely than others. Body language speaks for itself; therefore, a friendly demeanor must be displayed, even when it is not the true feeling.

Flight of the Bumblebee (Disgruntle Parents)

Despite positive efforts, principals will sometimes encounter parents who are disgruntled and confrontational upon arrival to the school, resulting in interactions similar to those displayed in "Flight of the Bumblebee," an orchestral interlude in the opera, *The Tale of Tsar Saltan*. The opera is a story of a prince who is transformed into an insect so that he can surreptitiously search for his father. The up-tempo piece depicts the erratic behavior of the bumblebee's journey in which he lashes out and stings his enemies, the source of his sorrows. The frantic pace of the music and the chaotic flight pattern of the bumblebee demonstrate how easily parent interactions can escalate from normal to extreme levels. Although composed in 1900 and fiendishly complicated to play, the "Flight of the Bumblebee" remains prevalent in popular culture today as encounters with disgruntled parents are common to the school setting. Therefore, principals must become skillful negotiators who are able to navigate hostile situations and assuage inflammatory conditions. Gestures such as addressing a parent waiting in the lobby with *"Ma'am give me just a few minutes to finish up this conference, and I will be right with you"* or *"I know this is important to you and we are going to take care of it"* can calm an explosive situation.

It is also essential to train staff to use positive language when communicating with parents. If the school has a procedure in which parents are not allowed down the hall after the morning bell or during the uninterrupted reading block, staff should use language such as *"May I help you"* rather than *"You can't go the hall."* Both statements address the school procedures in which the parent cannot go down the hall. However, one cannot be misconstrued as rude while the other can.

During conferences, principals must always hear the parent out without interruption, keeping in mind that many times a response is not needed; it is only the parent's opinion. This is not a sign of agreement but an opportunity for the parent to air grievances. Sometimes to be heard is the only resolution that is sought. Often, principals have difficulty with what appears to be awkward silence; however, it is a virtue worth practicing. Listening may be the best strategy to use with an irate parent who has already decided that they are absolute in their opinions. When they have exhausted their grievance, the principal should calmly implement the district policy or school procedure.

Timing and intuition are everything. At no point should an administrator argue with a parent. Intuitive principals read the room and take inventory of behaviors to assess the direction of the conference. They are alerted to behaviors such as the parent's refusal to sit or erratic behavior such as yelling, using profane language, displaying threatening body language, or making verbal threats. It is strongly recommended to have a witness when meeting with disgruntled parents. It is also imperative to keep detailed written notes from the conference for future reference as it not unusual for disgruntle parents to attempt to supersede the authority of the principal by seeking satisfaction from a superior, an acquaintance within the district, or through advocacies and legal avenues. Ultimately, all visitors are required to abide by board policy and school procedures; therefore, conferences that are disruptive to the school process should be discontinued.

The Bridge (Difficult Conversations)

The *bridge* is defined as a transition that takes the listener from one part of the music to the next. The bridge connects parents and the school to a common cause. Inherently, parents want what is best for their children, as does the school. This should be the philosophical framework for all communications. The disconnect happens when parents' expectations do not align with those of the school, and they fail to see that their child cannot be the exception to the rule when it comes to policy and procedures. The principal must explain the overall benefit of the code of conduct. Inappropriate behavior that goes

unchecked produces a chaotic environment that is negative for all children, including theirs.

When a student violates procedures, some parents
look for loopholes in the committed offense by making
statements such as, *"What about the time..." or "He wasn't
the only one..."* Principals cannot allow this type of mud-
dying the water. A separate investigation and conference
should be scheduled to address unrelated allegations.
Due to the contentious nature of discipline conferences,
it is best to get written statements from all parties involved immediately, as stories tend to change when
others get involved. Parents may also make demands
to know the discipline outcomes for other students. It is
understandable that they want fair treatment for their
child, but this cannot include a breach of confidentiality
in which the school discusses matters concerning other
students. In such incidences, the principal can only offer
the assurance that procedures are enforced equitably in
the school. The principal may also gingerly emphasize
that the parent's investment in their child's appropriate
behavior is an investment in the future. The school will
only interact with their child for a short period of time.

There are times that relationships between teachers
and parents become irreparable. When conversations become toxic and personal instead of productive, the principal will have to intervene and determine if a resolution
can be reached. Sometimes unfounded allegations become detrimental to the teacher's well-being and places
their livelihood and mental health in jeopardy. A decision to move the student's placement to another class-

room assignment may be the only alternative. Although most teachers are hesitant to inherit a disgruntled parent, a grade-level colleague may have to *take one for the team*. Colleagues must understand that this practice will be used with great discretion. It allows the parent and student to have a fresh start and places the school at an advantage if allegations continue. Making the same complaints from teacher to teacher loses credibility. Principals should keep detailed documentation of parent complaints.

The Chorus (Sharing Data)

Parents are partners in education; therefore, the home-school relationship should be indicative of a *chorus* performance in which there is unison in efforts to promote student achievement. Opportunities for two-way communication should be provided. In most instances, two conferences per year with the parent or guardian is usually acceptable. The teacher should utilize their expertise to share concerns with parents. It is always best to begin each conference on a positive note by discussing the student's favorable attributes. The parent should be given a chance to share concerns they may have first. With pertinent data in hand, the teacher should then get to the purpose of the conference. If the conference involves the student's behavior, anecdotal notes and other strategies must be available.

Parent-school collaborations include sharing data during conferences, open house, parental involvement day, honors assemblies, and other parent meetings. Traditionally, data is presented using graphs and tables; however, creating data movies with *animated gifs* promote excitement and places achievement at its rightful place, which is the forefront of the school program. Infinite themes may be used, such as sports, children's movies, careers, superheroes, etc. Educational accomplishments should rival the excitement of sports and other activities. Parents become more connected when they are aware of the school's academic performance. They are also more likely to return for parent meetings in the future.

The Interlude (Written Communications)

When there is an *interlude* or interruption which prohibits the principal or teacher from speaking directly with parents, written communications are often used. All written communications must be edited prior to sending to parents, as it is a form of documentation. This includes those sent by teachers and principals. Each teacher should have a partner editor on campus. Sometimes in haste, educators do not review written communications for content, spelling, and grammar. If time does not permit a response, it is best to acknowledge receipt and address the issue later. Teachers must be mindful that much can be lost in translation when using communication methods such as text messages and emails. Often, the written message is not interpreted as intended; therefore, directly speaking to parents lessens miscommunications. Social media can also be a doubled-edge sword. Whereas it is a good marketing and communication tool, it is also used in negative ways such as venting and as a platform to defame others out of anger. Teachers must be careful about responding to disgruntled parents about matters on social media. What is said on and off-campus must adhere to the district's standard of professionalism.

Each school decides when and how often communications are sent to parents. It is recommended that teachers send communications at least once per week and the principal once per month. *Communication folders* allow parents to receive essential information in a standard delivery format. The frequency of the messages should be carefully considered. Too many messages will give the impression that none are important.

Because teachers have busy schedules and many demands on their time, organizational tools are necessary to respond to the needs of parents without infringing on employee's immediate duties and responsibilities. A *Teacher Message Form* is an effective way to communicate parents' requests by allowing the teacher to respond conveniently. A *Request for Principal Conference Form* serves the same function. Many times, parents bring classroom issues directly to administrators without discussing them with the teacher. This requires several meetings and phone calls to bring the principal up to speed on issues. The principal conference form requires the parent to write the nature of the issue and efforts made to resolve it with the teacher. This provides fact-finding time for the principal. The parent can select potential dates and times that are convenient to hold a conference.

Principals must be open and accessible to parents; however, this is sometimes in direct conflict with acting as the instructional leader. Education must be the main priority while assuring parents that their concerns are important, as well. Every effort should be made to return calls by the end of the day. The office staff needs to be trained to discern situations that need immediate attention and those that can be addressed at a later time. It is imperative to know the audience. It may be more beneficial to address some requests sooner than others to keep issues from escalating, especially in cases of ongoing feuds between families and specific groups.

Administrators must also respond to employees regularly. Again, an open-door policy is desirable but not always practical. An *Employee Request Form* will allow the principal to respond to the many issues that arise. However, if the assignment is new, it is best to build relationships with employees and parents before utilizing an appointment system. This will avoid giving the appearance of being inaccessible or aloof, something that is not easily retracted.

Finally, communication can make or break a principal in the wake of tragedy, adversity, and negative relationships with staff and others. Therefore, it is more about *how* something is said rather than *what* was said. Discretions must be utilized at all times. Many school systems have a public relations person or agency appointed to speak to the public on behalf of the district during controversial situations. Sometimes, it is okay to pass the baton to the experts concerning unusual situations. Nevertheless, the principal will always be the face and spokesperson of the school.

Chapter Five

Ain't No Mountain High Enough

Organizing for Results

An artist may dream of being a superstar from a young age; however, it is the sweat equity that will determine whether this comes to fruition. Planning starts early. Many artists begin singing in churches, schools, and at local events. Eventually, they will intensify their efforts by studying with a voice coach, acquiring a manager to promote their career, and singing at larger venues. Their success does not come by happenstance but through grit, planning, and dedication to the craft. By the same token, organizing for results takes systematic planning, which encompasses the total school program. What educators believe about teaching and learning is crucial. That is, the school's belief system and whether educators take ownership of what and how much students learn will be a determining factor of its success.

One of the greatest challenges is to avoid giving into circumstances. This is sometimes easier said than done when schools are plagued with barriers to achievement. Educators must avoid the temptation to surrender to the barriers and disappointments that lead to negative thoughts, stereotypes, and actions. It is a fact that school programs face challenges in regard to student achievement. A challenge is defined as *a dare or call to take part in a contest or competition.* In education, the answer to that challenge must be a resounding, *I accept*. Achievement is not a matter of sport but rather a contest in which schools must be victorious; therefore, principals must organize for results to ensure success.

Concert Tickets (Buy-In)

The more a fan enjoys or believes in an artist's music, the more tickets he or she will buy. Therefore, success depends largely on the number of records and concert tickets sold. This kind of buy-in of the school's vision and mission also determines the school program's success. Buy-in includes a balance of ownership, commitment, and efficacy which tend to fluctuate as schools attempt to meet accountability standards. Therefore, the principal must promote or sell a *sense of urgency* for academic achievement to help combat the issue. A sense of urgency does not mean that teachers should be alarmed but consider the significant impact *every* decision has on student achievement. The intention is to reignite the purpose, passion, and calling within each teacher. Schools with a sense of urgency *A.I.M.* instruction by demonstrating heightened *awareness* of their role as change agents, being *intentional* in their actions, and using data to *measure* student achievement.

To create a heightened *awareness*, the principal must once again take the stage and appeal to teachers on a personal level through presentations that deepen their understanding of the work that must be done. This process begins with reflections of the power teachers have in impacting students' lives. Like an artist hired to perform at a once-in-a-lifetime event such as a wedding, graduation, bar mitzvah, or inaugural ball, their performance is a once-in-a-lifetime event for the honoree (student); there are no do-overs. Therefore, failure to deliver results in ever-lasting repercussions for the students in the next grade levels, college, and career choices. This awareness helps teachers understand that they must be responsive to the students they teach and find ways to meet their individual needs.

Many times, educators' evaluation of students' abilities results in a dismal prognosis. However, when instruction is closely inspected, there are identifiable causal gaps in which actions and objectives do not align. Instruction may be intermittently delivered with a disproportional emphasis in one or two areas. The gap may include ineffective questioning or small group instruction. The disconnect can be narrowed by providing and then reinforcing specific criteria or *intentional* actions leading to student achievement. Continuous feedback from the principal and professional development demonstrations help teachers to cement research-based practices in their instruction.

Instructional Alignment for Reading

Whole Group Reading	Small-Group Reading
Rigorous instruction based on standards	*Consistent and targeted*
Balances the five components of reading	*Appropriate modeling*

Builds background knowledge	Addresses deficient prerequisite skills
Promotes critical thinking	Reinforces previous concepts
Students conduct cursory read to examine text	Provides guided practice
Higher-order questions that make connections to real-world experiences	Includes prepared examples (phonics patterns, sight words, vocabulary, and fluency)
Appropriate modeling and guided practice	Perky pace
Provides authentic reading opportunities	Interactive
Provides a perky pace of instruction	Provides authentic reading opportunities
Students interact to clarify understanding	Appropriate checking for understanding
Students summarize and provide evidence	Accountability
Written open-ended responses	
Effective checking for understanding	
Independent practice	

Instructional Alignment for Math

Whole Group Math	**Small-Group Math**
Rigorous instruction based on standards	Consistent and targeted
Builds on previous knowledge	Appropriate modeling
Promotes problem-solving	Addresses deficient prerequisite skills
Encourages multiple ways to solve problems	Reinforces previous concepts
Appropriate modeling and guided practice	Provides guided practice

Honors the process over answers	Perky pace
Uses math manipulatives appropriately	Interactive
Higher-order questions that make connections to real-world experiences	Includes prepared examples
Perky pace of instruction	Appropriate checking for understanding
Students interact to clarify understanding	Accountability
Students explain their thinking and work	
Written open-ended responses	
Effective checking for understanding	
Independent practice	

It is not enough to be aware and intentional, but understand that *teaching and learning have a reciprocal relationship.* One does not exist without the other. Schools must be mindful that the *measure* of effective teaching is student achievement and look to the data instead of applying subjective means that support feelings rather than facts. Instruction can look good on the surface yet yield poor data. This is especially difficult when the teacher appears to be doing a good job, but data suggests otherwise. Educators must learn to treat the product of student achievement in the same manner as society treats other goods and services. Customer satisfaction is a universal prime concern in which society places high expectations for services rendered. Paradoxically, education is one of a few fields in which the customer is expected to assume the responsibility for the finished product: achievement. Although there are extenuating circumstances—such as the students' starting point—when adequate growth is not achieved, the school should assume the responsibility and begin delving into *why*.

Sheet Music (Reading the Data)

Sheet music notates components of a song or musical piece. It must be followed meticulously as data must be followed to implement the improvement process. Analyzing data and conducting a needs assessment are the first steps of the process. Achievement, perception, and demographic data are reviewed to develop a comprehensive picture of the school. Achievement data must be triangulated for reliability and reviewed for possible trends. If several data points or assessments show the same deficiencies, this must be an area of focus.

Because of its importance, a data room is essential for every school. It is the school's boardroom where projections for the year are made based on previous performance. Data should be organized and displayed by school, grade level, and teachers. This helps teachers to see how their data feeds into the performance of the school. Monitoring or tracking charts of benchmark assessments or other school assessments provide a visual representation of students' progress by class. Generally, scale scores are monitored for growth.

Suppose students fail to make progress during the monitoring process. In that case, it is evident that they will not meet proficiency on high-stakes assessments. Therefore, principals must *inspect what they expect*. Data is useless if it is not used to drive instruction. Teachers should systematically review an array of data, including formative (common, benchmark, quarterly) and summative assessments. All meetings need to be led by the principal and the instructional leadership team. Gradebooks should be analyzed to determine the percent of proficient students rather than class averages, as they can be misleading. Students are individuals, and educators need to know how each is progressing. Data meeting forms that are designed to fit the assessment provide documentation of teacher and grade-level performance and strategies for improvement. Questions included on the data form should be written to evoke conversation among teachers to analyze student data by identifying areas in which students experience difficulties. Verbal discussion between colleagues is essential.

Beethoven's 5ᵗʰ (A Symphony of Strategies)

Beethoven composed nine symphonies amongst other pursuits during his career. With four distinguished opening notes, the *5ᵗʰ Symphony* is arguably the most recognizable. It is frequently sampled in today's music, as well as used in the television and movie industry. Although this masterpiece reached critical acclaim, it took Beethoven from 1804-1808 to complete it. The first performance was not well received due to lack of rehearsals and mistakes made during the concert. Beethoven also endured a difficult and sometimes abusive childhood, and eventually lost his hearing in his mid-30s. Through it all, he remained steadfast in his creative endeavors, proving that dedication and perseverance can overcome adversity.

Creativity is not just a phenomenon found in the world of music, and neither is adversity. Schools must creatively develop a *symphony* of strategies to remove barriers to achievement, especially as it relates to meeting state accountability standards. As with the case of Beethoven's first performance of the 5th *Symphony*, the way strategies are implemented will ultimately determine their success. The most prevalent of these strategies is *extended day tutoring,* which extends learning beyond the regular school day. This activity is usually funded through Title I. Schools must decide what criteria will be used to select students.

Although it is common to select only students with the lowest performance in reading and math, offering the service to students who need extra support may reduce the number of students who will fall into the intensive range if help is not received. Tutoring with a very low ratio (6:1) is most effective. The tutoring materials need to be closely aligned to the curriculum that students engage in during the regular school day. The classroom teacher needs to provide a weekly list of specific deficient skills for students in tutoring and engage in two-way communication with the tutor to ensure a successful program. Administrators and teachers should track student performances quarterly to determine growth.

Extended day tutoring may be further implemented

through *Saturday Boot Camp*. The boot camp is a half-day intensive approach to closing the achievement gap in reading and math. Each Saturday, teachers deliver a variety of skills and test-taking strategies designed to help students perform better on standardized or accountability assessments. A status report which informs parents of how close or far away their child is to reaching their goal for the high-stakes assessment should be sent home with each student. This can be an eye-opener and an incentive for parents to grant permission for students to attend. This strategy should be implemented far enough in advance to make an impact on student performance, but not so far in advance that they will experience burnout. The camp should focus on targeted skills but also offer enrichment such as friendly competitions or online instructional games.

Accelerated Learning Academies (ALA or Academy) is an improvement strategy that targets the above-average learner. Due to accountability, an enormous amount of time is spent providing intervention for students who have subject matter deficiencies. This has created a conundrum when it comes to addressing the needs of students who do not experience academic difficulties and those who would benefit from a more advanced curriculum. Frequently, they are not afforded an equitable education based on their needs. Many receive a sort of *fast food* or *leftover* education based on the limited amount of time that remains after re-teaching and intervention. Others serve as peer tutors to their classmates. Whereas student collaborations are beneficial to both parties, advanced students are disadvantaged when competing globally, resulting in a *big fish in a little pond* phenomenon. It may appear that they are doing well when compared to peers in their school, but this may not be the case according to state or national norms. As a result, it is not uncommon for some to perform below proficient on state assessments. The rigor of instruction for these students needs to be increased to expand their horizons and become truly college and career-ready.

The Accelerated Learning Academy concept is a strategy that may be used to ensure that high achievers make significant progress while engaging in enrichment activities. Students are expected to excel in their studies and represent the school at the highest level of achievement on state and district assessments. The principal may begin by creating one *Academy Class* per grade level with the goal of increasing that number in subsequent years. The classes do not significantly impact the heterogeneous schema set forth by most districts but provide a platform for all students to be successful.

Students are matched with teachers who are driven, self-starters, technologically savvy, and enjoy the challenge of thinking outside of the box. They engage in rigorous lessons that allow them to reach their optimal potential. *Academy Classes* also serve as a solution to the exodus of public school students to private, parochial, and charter schools. Parents of advanced students constantly seek special opportunities and options for their children. Activities such as cultural studies, foreign language, research projects, and advanced studies found in *Academy Classes* are among those options.

Student *goal cards* are another effective strategy that allows students to take ownership of their learning by setting achievement goals they wish to attain. Students monitor their progress on benchmark assessments by recording their progress on *goal cards* that are taped to their desks. The visual promotes intrinsic motivation and self-evaluations. The teacher should hold conferences with each student to discuss their progress. A variety of class charts such as thermometers, checklists, etc. are also utilized to display the class performance. This helps to keep the class focused and their eyes on the prize. It also encourages students to do their part as a class community member. The teacher may set up rewards as the class reaches a milestone.

In addition to strategies that are implemented at school, teachers should solicit commitment from parents to ensure daily practice to *close the achievement gap. Close the gap* activities are folder activities sent home for students to practice for an extended period of time. This activity does not take the place of regular homework. Still, it is an ongoing strategy designed to eliminate interferences to learning higher-order concepts.

Curriculum Addendums have been used in a variety of ways and are very effective in improving student achievement. This may be accomplished by adding or pacing skills that will not be taught until the fourth quarter into the first through third quarters to assure that they are addressed prior to high stakes testing. Common deficient skills may be allotted in the same manner. Using past data, it can be determined which standards or objectives will need the most attention. This may mean using a daily focus such as a bell ringer to address the skills throughout the year, even though they may not be tested until later.

Teachers must also discern, if possible, the number of item types are on accountability assessments which will assist in determining how much emphasis should be placed on each. Many assessments have item specifications that will help with this process. Suppose an assessment has one or two items on a particular standard and ten on another. In that case, teachers must understand that a disproportionate amount of time on the former will not yield proficiency overall. There are skills in each school in which students have historically performed deficiently. These should be given priority.

Test prep activities are also instrumental in student achievement. *A test prep period* added to schedules by mid-year is impactful as high stakes tests approach. During this time, teachers focus on test-taking strategies. The schedule includes activities such as mini-lessons on a variety of skills. The goal is to activate knowledge from lessons previously taught since students sometimes retain information in their short-term memory. Test preparation may include other activities such as keyboarding and open-ended responses, as well.

Hosting a *Test Prep Olympics* gets students motivated to perform at their best level. The Test Prep Olympics is a grade-level competition with games such as *Number Sense High Jump* in which students answer computer-based questions about understanding numbers, *Basic Facts Relay* (multiplication and division problems), *Brain Hurdles* (computer-based vocabulary questions), *Morphology Long Jump* (matching word forms to their meanings), *Analogy Javelin* (analogy questions), and *Math Triathlon* (solving multi-step word problems). Teachers create the teams and content for games. A study guide in which students can earn extra points is sent home before the Olympics. The points are added to the class's total score. Trophies and medals are given to the winning class on each grade level. Students who do not take the accountability assessment serve as the audience to cheer for their peers.

Academic Pep Rallies go hand in hand with motivating students. Each class performs a song or chant of their creation during this event in which the winning classes receive a trophy. This gives students and teachers an opportunity to display their school spirit prior to testing. Teachers may also get involved by participating in a *Critical Thinking Fashion Show* in which they model decorative sashes highlighting critical thinking words. As teachers model, the narrator reads the *runway* description of the word such as *analyze* or *compare.* The purpose is to remind students how to utilize higher-order thinking to improve comprehension during the assessment.

Maintaining student morale while taking difficult assessments for long durations can be an arduous task. Teachers must employ strategies to increase students' stamina by providing rigorous practice tasks, timing work assignments, and providing effective modeling.

Playing motivational songs each morning of testing such as "Champion" by Carrie Underwood, featuring Ludacris, "Best Day of My Life" by American Authors, and "Superheroes" by the Script set the stage for success and help to calm nerves - teachers and students. Distributing rewards on the day of the assessment is also an effective way to motivate students. Rewards may include a *We're on Fire Day* (Hot Fries), *Proud as a Pickle Day* (Pickles), *Hot Diggity Dog Day* (Hot Dogs and drinks), and *Cool Achievers Day* (Kool Pops). Students must earn a ticket from their teacher in order to participate. The ticket is awarded to students who focused and put forth their best effort. It is not based on performance.

A New Song (A Paradigm Shift)

Many times artists introduce new songs as part of their line-up that may not be fan favorites. The reason is obvious. Whereas fans love to hear the old signature songs, artists need to promote new material to continue their livelihood. To be successful, schools must continue to evolve, as well, to keep up with the demands of the 21st century. Innovation is often suggested, yet when it comes to addressing certain issues, it is often business as usual, as evidenced in underprivileged schools plagued with issues such as achievement, staffing, resources, and behavior. Staffing issues can be addressed by establishing a cadre of highly skilled teachers to employ in hard-to-staff schools. Of course, employees must be given an incentive for their expertise. The reality is teachers are not lining up to teach in schools besieged with behavior and academic issues resulting in the hiring of newly, untrained, or ineffective teachers. This perpetuates a cycle of failure.

Teachers with a proven record should be recruited to close this gap. Extensive professional development for instruction, culture and climate, and classroom management must be provided. Similarly, the issue with providing substitute teachers for these schools must be addressed. By creating a group of capable and centralized substitutes designated to serve underprivileged schools, principals will not have to use unorthodox means to cover classes when teachers are absent. Solutions sometimes involve the principal holding classes herself, among many other duties.

When administrators are overburdened in this manner, they are less effective in promoting the school program. Principal mentors can be a great asset to helping those in need meet their responsibilities, especially if the mentee is made part of the selection process. The mentor should possess expertise in related areas in need of improvement. This may include good human-relation skills, curriculum, data analysis, etc. By matching mentees with successful principals with similar administrative backgrounds, the collaboration is made more effective.

Chapter Six
<u>Higher Ground</u>
Professional Development

Musicians are constantly looking to professionally develop or enhance their craft. It may mean adding a little rap to their music, auto-tunes, or collaborating with another musician. Just like educators, they are continuously attempting to reinvent themselves in order to stay relevant. Teachers also must engage in meaningful professional development to stay relatable to students. While this does not mean they have to be their students' best friends, they will have to put forth the effort to connect with them. This includes knowing interests and talents and spicing up lessons by keeping abreast of current trends in education, entertainment, and technology. Teachers and administrators who are viewed as outdated will have a more difficult time reaching their students.

Instruction must incorporate a variety of current and effective strategies to motivate students and maximize learning. To become an expert at anything requires practice and practice makes perfect. To become an expert in education, one must be an ongoing learner. Teachers become highly qualified leaders in their field because they are dedicated to continuous learning. The *Glossary of Education Reform* defines professional development as a wide variety of specialized training, formal education, or advanced professional learning intended to help administrators, teachers, and other educators improve their professional knowledge, competence skills, and effectiveness. Professional development encompasses a wide range of knowledge that is essential to performing educational duties. To master the art of teaching and learning and become expert practitioners, teachers must engage in professional development and reflect on their practices in accordance with research such as the *National Board for Professional Teaching Standards (NBPTS)*. The *Board* has five core propositions:

1. *Proposition One*: teachers are committed to students and their learning.
2. *Proposition Two*: teachers know the subject they teach and how to teach those subjects to students.
3. *Proposition Three*: teachers are responsible for managing and monitoring student learning.
4. *Proposition Four*: teachers think systematically about their practices and learn from experience.
5. *Proposition Five:* teachers are members of learning communities.

At its core, professional development is a commitment to student learning, as teachers refine their practices. It begins with an awareness of legislature pertaining to education.

The Bar (School Law and Policies)

The *bar* (sometimes referred to as measures) determines the rhythm of the song. The bar governs the number of beats and the value of the note in each song which greatly affects the sound. Knowing this helps the musician play music correctly. School law and policies govern education and ensure that decisions are equitable, fair, and legal. Principals and staff must be familiar with legislature and policies that affect the everyday operations of the school. Their success will be measured by their understanding and implementation. The first of which is ESSA (*Every Student Succeed Act, 2015*). This law specifically outlines a number of provisions for education:

1. equity for disadvantaged children,
2. high academic standards that prepare students to be college and career ready,
3. reporting of student progress through statewide assessments,
4. innovation in schools,
5. expansion of high-quality preschool
6. improvement in low performing schools and low graduation rates

Laws such as ESSA provide the framework for accountability and educating students. It replaced the No Child Left Behind Act of 2002.

At a minimum, teachers and principals must also have an understanding of freedoms afforded to all citizens in the United States. The *Fourteenth Amendment* grants equal rights and protections under the law. Many school-related lawsuits come under this umbrella, especially as it relates to special needs students and minorities. It is the cornerstone for discrimination cases such as the Supreme

Court case of *Brown v. the Board of Education of Topeka (1954)*. This decision ruled that racial segregation was unconstitutional. Segregation as a legal practice, for the most part, is a thing of the past. Discriminatory practices as they relate to enrollment, due process, suspensions, hiring practices, termination practices, etc., are not. Title IX also addresses civil rights by prohibiting discrimination based on sex, in education programs that receive federal financial assistance.

It is a part of the Education Amendments of 1972 but has gained attention due to the growing transgender community. School officials must also be knowledgeable of *Public Law 94-142 (PL 94-142)* of the *Education for All Handicapped Children Act (EAHCA) of 1975*. This case protects the rights of individuals with disabilities. It also ensures a "free, appropriate public education." It affects decisions related to student placement, facility use, transportation, inclusion in school-related events such as field trips and clubs, as well as many other implications.

The *First Amendment* grants rights to free speech and peaceful assembly. In *Tinker v. Des Moines Independent School District (1969)*, high school students were suspended for wearing armbands to protest the Vietnam War. The Supreme Court upheld their actions and affirmed that "students do not shed their constitutional rights to freedom of speech and expression at the schoolhouse gate." However, speech that is lewd or disruptive to the school process *can* be prohibited. In addition, this amendment protects the right to religious freedom and the right not to practice religion at all. It also encompasses freedom of expression cases involving dress codes, hairstyles, tattoos, etc. Much of the controversies in schools involve *First Amendment* rights. Administrators should use court precedents when deciding to pursue issues related to *First Amendment* rights. This will help determine if doing so is a worthwhile endeavor.

The *Fourth Amendment (1791)* outlines guidelines for lawful search and seizures. Cases involving search and seizure must pass a litmus test of reasonability; that is, the search must be justifiable *at the inception*. The school must have reasons that would justify their actions, which does not include an arbitrary or random search. In the case *New Jersey v. T.L.O. (1985)*, the Supreme Court ruled that the school was justified in searching a 14-year-old female's purse when there was evidence that she and another student were smoking in the restroom.

Meeting the burden of reasonability has become less difficult in light of school shootings. Courts are more apt to rule in favor of schools due to safety issues. In addition to the aforementioned, schools must have a basic understanding of tort law in which plaintiffs sue for monetary gain. Cases include negligence, injury, and emotional distress, among others. Schools and districts are highly susceptible to such lawsuits.

Educators need not become lawyers but possess a fundamental understanding of laws, landmark cases, and policies when making decisions. Principals and staff must also be aware of and follow district policies to fidelity, especially regarding the code of conduct, safety, and treatment of students.

Jam Sessions (data meetings, instructional delivery, and book studies)

Jam sessions provide an opportunity for musicians to practice new progressions and arrangements of music in a professional learning community. The jam sessions may be formal or informal with no pre-determined goal. Educational jam sessions allow colleagues to fine-tune their practices and learn from each other; however, unlike musical jam sessions, educational jam sessions must have a predetermined goal that focuses on the needs of the school. *Educational jam sessions* or *Professional development can usually be characterized as three types; data meetings, instructional delivery, or book studies.*

Instrumental Professional Development (Data Meetings)

Discussed previously, data meetings are *instrumental professional development* essential to effective instruction. Data meetings accompany all other professional development by determining the needs of the school. When data is analyzed, strategies are developed for improvement, and outcomes are tracked and monitored. Teachers are then able to adjust instruction and close achievement gaps. Professional development is also driven by observations of instruction, school culture and climate, as well as school, district, and state initiatives or policies.

Principals should determine the types of training the

staff has had and then conduct several walk-throughs to see the day-to-day implementation by looking for explicit reading instruction both whole and small group. A well-designed reading walk-through form can be used to start this process. Teachers should be observed implementing strategies learned in previous training, followed by constructive feedback notes from the observation. The principal will then have a better idea of where to begin providing professional development. Coaches should be informed of what needs to be addressed and follow up in a timely manner to see if the improvement is made. This method offers the best results for improving teacher instruction. The process is time-consuming, however quite beneficial. The same process needs to be used for ensuring explicit math instruction for students. School-wide professional development for initiatives needs to be determined after working with staff for at least a year. This way, a more knowledgeable decision can be made. Programs will not change the instructional environment by themselves.

Classical Professional Development (Instructional Delivery)

Classical or traditional professional development in education includes reading, writing, mathematics, and all other subjects. Professional development should be designed to help teachers eliminate misconceptions and implement instruction effectively such as knowing how to respond when students cannot read fluently. Fluency journals which include poems, songs, and passages are an easy way to increase fluency. Poems and songs have a natural rhythm that makes it easy for students to predict what word comes next, which makes it easier to practice reading for word recognition.

Although comprehension is paramount, students must be able to recognize words in order to comprehend. Fluency journal activities cover an array of word study skills that are often found in poems and songs. Teachers should not forget that the best way to improve fluency is by allotting time for students to read at school and promoting reading at home. There is no substitute; hence the maxim, *Good Readers, Read.* Vocabulary and word study skills help students comprehend what they read, as well as read more fluently. Students with extensive instruction in morphology are able to attack unknown vocabulary words with greater ease. Greek and Latin roots cover a wide range of vocabulary. When students understand their meanings, it may be applied to new situations. Placing emphasis on affixes will also yield positive results when analyzing vocabulary.

Comprehension training assists teachers in how to approach a variety of texts, including fiction and non-fiction. This will help students navigate and understand essential elements such as vocabulary, main idea, supporting details, cause and effect, author's purpose, context clues, etc. Students are taught to make inferences and cite evidence to defend their answers. The process includes comparing texts and having students extend learning through open-ended writing assignments related to the text.

Professional development that addresses writing

helps teachers to develop norms for assessing student work. By using grade-level rubrics, teachers are able to calibrate the grading process, thereby ensuring equity. If this is not done, teachers will subjectively grade students' writings by sometimes inserting feelings about what they think the student knows or is trying to say rather than what they are actually saying. Each teacher grades a high, medium, and low student work sample during professional development. Afterward, they complete their finding and assign a grade according to the rubric (on a separate sheet). Students' names should remain anonymous. Teachers exchange the writing sample with co-workers to grade, as well. The samples are passed until all teachers have graded all samples. They then discuss their findings and calibrate the grading process. This helps to refine the assessment of students' writing.

Mathematics professional development addresses an array of standards and should be centered around problem-solving in which students build conceptual understanding and relate math to the real world using manipulatives (real and virtual). Students learn to analyze and solve problems without relying on algorithms. A key component of mathematics professional development is for teachers to learn skills needed to facilitate learning by helping students recognize misconceptions and make connections between concepts. Science and social studies professional development allow teachers to create lessons to help students make real life application of concepts.

Popular Professional Development (Book Studies)

Popular professional development address those issues that are unique within each school. Book studies can be used to explore popular topics based on the needs and desires of the school. What may be popular or prevalent in one school may not be in another. Books such as *Fish* by Stephen C. Lundin, *Peaks and Valleys* and *Who Moved My Cheese* by Spencer Johnson, not only improve morale, but have an incidental benefit of improving instruction and interactions with students.

Fish is a fictional story about improving negative behaviors such as apathy, low morale, low productivity, and burnout in the workplace. *Peaks and Valleys* is a fable that teaches how to handle obstacles and adversity that will be encountered in life. *Who Moved My Cheese* is a must-read for administrators needing to make changes in the school program. This book helps to bridge the gap of going from old to new. *Teach Like a Pirate* by Dave Burgess encourages teachers to use their passion and talents to bring their classroom instruction to life. Other books such as the *5 Practices for Orchestrating Productive Mathematics Discussions* by Margaret S. Smith and Mary Kay Stein focus on building conceptual understanding by helping students facilitate their own learning through five sequential steps.

Book study protocols may vary from traditional methods of small or whole discussion to variations such as skits, responses through technology, or specifically designed modules. *Digital presentation modules* help to maximize the benefit of book studies. The modules include the following components: *overview, outcomes, activation, engagement, reflection, and link:*

1. During the *overview*, presenters introduce the book, set norms, and explain the format or delivery. This often includes background information.
2. Next, the *expected outcomes* of the book study are discussed. What will be accomplished as a result of the book study? How does it relate to job performance?
3. The *activation* phase introduces and extends concepts by using short video clips or other methods that best exemplifies the author's message.
4. During the *engagement* phase, teachers peruse specific sections as a review.
5. The *reflection* phase includes writing and sharing individual reflections by completing the following phrases: The text says… and this reminds me of….
6. The *link* phase provides an opportunity for teachers to summarize concepts and make connections from the text to school-related topics. This phase may be completed individually but is often completed in groups.

The following pages contain sample modules that may be used to conduct book studies.

Book Study Module 1

More Than A Bird by Liz Huntley

Overview: Introduce norms, format, and provide context for book study. Ex: *More Than a Bird* is an autobiography of a little girl who experienced a traumatic childhood and found refuge in school at an early age. Provide statistics for at-risk students.

Outcomes: Identify signs of at-risk students and develop strategies to build rapport.

Activate: Presenters explain the precarious nature of identifying at-risk students using short, applicable video clips from *Annie (2014)*. In the movie, the lead character possesses a vivacious personality that does not align with expected behavior of an at-risk student. In the book, the character showed similar qualities; however, there were other common similarities, good and bad. Complete Venn diagram comparing and contrasting Annie with the main character.

Extend concept through group activity, *Anatomy of a Child* (use large graphic outline of a child). Each group will think of words that describe students in their classroom or the main character and write characteristics on body parts, placing the most favorable characteristic at the core (torso). Although students may come with some challenges, they also possess other valuable and admirable qualities. Ex: The main character in the book was *apprehensive* (head), she felt *invisible*, yet *hopeful* (arms), she was *reflective*, yet felt *unworthy* (legs), and at the core, she was extremely *intelligent* (torso). Groups present and explain their selections. Other potential descriptors include *determined, creative, responsible, traumatized, dedicated, studious, gifted, overwhelmed, distrusting, talented, uncertain, challenged, resilient, broken, impoverished, distressed, thoughtful, temperamental, disobedient, naughty, delinquent, mischievous, unruly, disorderly, aggressive, anxious, malnourished, angry, overactive, and hypersensitive.*

Engage: Peruse and review specified sections of the book.

Reflect: Use form to write individual reflections to explain how the new information relates to past experiences. The text says… and this reminds me of… Share reflections.

Link: Complete link activity by incorporating article on trauma-sensitive students. Identify strategies of support and discuss negative triggers. Brainstorm solutions to address common behaviors of at-risk students.

Book Study Module 2

Fish by Stephen Lundin

Overview: Introduce norms, format, and provide context for book study. Ex: Fish is based on the productive atmosphere of the Seattle Fish Market. Show video clip of Seattle Fish Market and discuss the level of morale. Share workplace satisfaction statistics and discuss the need for a positive school climate.

Outcomes: Identify and develop strategies that promote a positive work environment, promote job satisfaction and increase productivity.

Activate: Use short, applicable video clips from *The Devil Wears Prada* to explain the section of the book that refers to *Choose Your Attitude.* Pertinent clips are demonstrative of how *attitude affect performance.* The main character blamed her boss for her misery and lack of success in a job at an upscale fashion magazine while in actuality, she only accepted the job to boost her career as a *serious* journalist, something that she did not view the fashion industry as being. She realized that her attitude toward the business was holding her back proving that how circumstances are viewed may be more powerful than the circumstances themselves.

Engage: Teachers engage with the text by perusing the *Choose Your Attitude* section.

Reflect: Write reflections describing an incident in which you or someone you know changed their attitude with positive results. Ex: The text says… and this reminds me of…

Link: After discussing how attitudes are a matter of choice, teachers will complete the link activity, *Sounds Fishy to Me.* Each group is given a scenario in which the employee is dissatisfied with a school-related situation. They will develop an alternate view which persuades the employee to change her mind. Ex: learning a new initiative, writing explicit lesson plans, referring a student who misbehaves, but is not suspended, doing duty, dealing with unsupportive parents, administering accountability assessments, using manipulatives during math instruction, addressing students who fail to complete homework, or using technology during instruction, etc.

Professional Development Itinerary (Where, How, When)

Professional development requires a significant amount of planning. Factors include securing the studio space (where), deciding the method of delivery (how), and scheduling the time (when). There are several methods to deliver training, including that which is delivered through conferences, district training, and embedded at the local school. Conferences offer a vast range of professional training to meet the needs and interests of teachers by providing an opportunity to learn innovative practices from colleagues across the country. The obvious drawback to this method is the cost of registration, accommodation, substitutes, and travel. Training offered by districts is more feasible, especially as it relates to new initiatives, assessments, or text book series.

The goal is to equip teachers with the necessary skills to implement the programs with fidelity. The training may include the use of consultants or district personnel. Many times, it is conducted over the summer, which can sometimes hinder implementation as teachers do not apply what is learned immediately. This may result in faulty implementation, in which case it will be the principal's responsibility to provide support. In addition, the district usually has departments to aid when requested.

The most prevalent form of professional development is *embedded professional development* which can be delivered at the local school. *Side-by-side coaching* for reading and math is a good place to start, if there is a reading and/or math coach on staff. If not, this may become the responsibility of the reading and math lead teachers. While this method is successful, it is limited by the number of teachers who can be served at a given time. Suppose the staff is new staff or has copious needs. In that case, coaches will have difficulty meeting all of their needs through the coaching cycle, which includes one-on-one planning sessions, side-by-side coaching, and debriefing. Whole group presentations or *demonstration lessons* may be used as a supplement. It provides a birds-eye view of instructional delivery and an opportunity to ask clarifying questions. The leadership team or teachers determine topics of interest to be presented to the staff.

Professional development may also include *videotaped lessons* for delivery to a larger audience. This saves a lot of time and is very impactful. Teachers should be given an observation form to take notes to be discussed at the end of the lesson. It is imperative that they activate their knowledge by participating in the discussion and asking and answering questions. This activity may be reversed by having teachers videotape themselves and critique the lesson with a building coach. As a follow-up, grade levels may request which skills they would like for the coaches to address for upcoming professional development. *Webinars* or *webcasts* are also a popular and cost-saving method of professional development.

In addition, teachers may train other teachers by *Skyping* from class to class. This gives the mentee a chance to see the mentor's interaction with students, preferably on the same grade level. The principal needs to make sure that the methods being employed are effective by making the ultimate decision of which teacher will be observed. Again, debriefing is a necessary step. A similar method is to develop classrooms for *site studies*. Teachers who have expertise in certain areas are trained to help teachers who need support. The principal arranges for a substitute for a full or partial day so that the mentee can shadow a mentor. The principal and teacher should discuss the purpose of the observation upfront. An observation form should be completed, and debriefing should take place within two days.

Many districts require teachers to complete a *professional learning plan*. Teachers determine what standards they would like to address for the year. This is submitted to the principal for approval. However, some principals utilize school-wide professional learning plans, which include new initiatives or school-wide focuses such as the use of authentic technology, diversity, reading and math instruction, etc. This enables the teacher to concentrate their efforts. The principal determines which strategies will be included and the evidence that will be submitted. Evidence should always include qualitative data such as reflections and quantitative data such as benchmark assessment results. Teachers are permitted to choose additional areas of focus.

There are several models that principals may use to

schedule weekly, bi-weekly, or monthly professional development. The first includes designating a day in which *vertical teams* such as K-2 and 3-5 meet once per week. This method requires planning and funding (Title I or Title II). For weekly professional development, substitutes commit to work a flip schedule on the designated day of each week for the duration of the year. Friday is a good day since it is typically a wind-down day. It also helps to increase teacher attendance as they look forward to interacting with their peers on a professional level. This method also decreases the need for weekly afternoon faculty meetings and provides more collaboration time for teachers. It is accomplished by hosting a character assembly to engage students while teachers participate in professional development. Again, specialty area teachers (counselor, P.E. coach, and media specialist) host the character assembly each Friday.

The counselor creates the schedule on the morning of training according to substitutes who are present. Other school employees may be utilized if there is a shortage. Typically, training begins at 8:30–11:00 for the first group and 12:00–2:30 for the second group. The *grade level model* is a variation used by commissioning fewer substitutes one to two times per week to rotate from grade level to grade level or scheduling grade level activities such as lunch, physical education, media lab, and computer lab (art, music, etc.) back-to-back on the same day. This enables the principal to host professional development for specific grade levels once per week. Usually, two grade levels per day can be accommodated with this method. Also, substitutes would not be required. Scheduling may also include extending physical education, media lab, computer lab, or other specialty activity once per week by 45 minutes to one hour, allowing additional time for professional development.

Demands on educators to meet student achievement goals have become increasingly challenging. Teachers must be competent to fulfill their professional responsibilities and implement new initiatives while maintaining a positive perspective. This requires ongoing strategic professional development planning.

Chapter Seven

Stop! In the Name of Love

Safe Learning Environment

Vocal groups are generally comprised of a lead singer and several background singers. When synchronized, they produce a unique sound. Although the background singers add value to the performance, the lead singer is usually the featured act of the group whose voice is paramount to its success. Fans would hardly notice if one of the background singers is missing during a concert. However, if the lead singer or main act were not to perform, the absence takes on a different meaning.

The importance of a safe and orderly environment holds a similar position in the school setting. It is supreme to the well-being of children. It supersedes academics and all other components; therefore, the chief concern of school administration should be promoting conditions that are safe and conducive to learning. By doing so, students flourish academically, emotionally, and socially, as commonly reflected in the school's mission and vision statement.

The principal must possess a certain amount of mastery in forecasting potential risks. Consistently accomplishing this task can be precarious in which the principal must balance an open school program for all stakeholders with external influences that threaten a safe environment. This has to be accomplished while under micro-scopic scrutiny from the media, as education is a topic that fuels politics and news. Every employee must know the proper procedure for every given situation. It should not vary from person to person. Students must also be aware of safety procedures which are outlined in school rules and the school-wide discipline plan.

Securing the Perimeter (Protocol and Classroom Management)

A major part of event planning includes *securing the perimeter* in which plans are made for the known and un-known. The safety plan and school-wide discipline plan serves this purpose in schools. The safety plan includes community resources and contact information in case of an emergency, such as local hospitals, law enforcement, public works, and social services. The plan also identi-fies the essential roles of staff members such as commu-nications liaison, student release coordinator, and triage leader, as well as a list of available on-site emergency equipment. The principal must ensure that all employ-ees are familiar with the plan and their role. An explic-itly written *school-wide discipline plan* helps students and parents understand expected behavior. Expectations for each area of the school should be listed and posted near applicable areas along with school-wide rules. Specifical-ly, the classroom, hallway, restroom, gym, playground, assembly, cafeteria, library, computer lab, science lab, bus, carline, and van area should be addressed.

Effectively planning and monitoring *morning and af-ternoon duties* help to keep students safe. Teachers must arrive in ample time before students. Some schools house students in the gym once they have eaten breakfast, while others send them to sit next to their classrooms with staff serving as hall monitors. Activities such as reading give students something to do as they wait for the bell. Teachers should exchange phone numbers with a colleague to replace them in case of an absence or late arrival. Afternoon duties must also be assigned as needed. The parent-student handbook should explain the late pick-up policy. Parents and daycare vans who pick children up late should be given a copy of the principal's *Late Pick-Up Letter*. The letter states the time and cost of the late pick-up. This will decrease the frequency of students left at the school after hours.

Classroom management skills can and often determine the success of a teacher. It affects student achievement and the ability to maintain an orderly environment. New teachers must be provided an orientation to explain the following: effective planning, time on task, student engagement, consistency, classroom management system (rewards and consequences), communication with parents, building a rapport with students, and using various resources. Elements of classroom management should be implemented *simultaneously*. Emphasizing one or two elements without consistency is a recipe for failure. Beginning the first day of school, teachers should introduce and reinforce rules frequently with the understanding that *consistency is imperative*. However, reinforcing rules alone is not enough.

Many teachers fail to understand the role that planning, rapport, engagement, and communication play in their success. Teachers who do not build relationships with their students or exhibit off-task behavior begin to have issues immediately. When students reject this idea and poor behavior increases, office discipline referrals increase. Sometimes, a small number of teachers are responsible for the greatest number of suspensions in the school. If not addressed, this may persist year after year.

Monthly *discipline data meetings* provide an opportunity to discuss classroom management techniques and provide an overview of data as it pertains to specific infractions, when and where those infractions occur, and office referrals and suspensions by grade level and teacher. The data can be used to initiate dialogue with teachers and to determine professional development needs. Teachers and students must display mutual respect in order to be productive. Unlike businesses that deal in goods, service-oriented organizations are characterized by human relationships. The better the relationship, the better the outcome for all parties. This concept extends to interactions with parents, as well.

Students with continued disruptive behavior will need more serious interventions such as a point card with 2-3 goals that the student will attempt to reach daily and a behavior management plan. For the point card, the type, frequency, and the time that the behavior occurs should be taken into consideration. The teacher should start with small intervals of time and increase as the student's behavior improves. The point card should be perceived as a positive intervention to encourage the student. The behavior management plan describes the behavior the student agrees to improve, criteria for success, and consequences and rewards. Teachers often consider point cards and behavior management plans as excessive work; however, they demonstrate the school's steps to assist the student and puts them one step closer to getting additional assistance, if needed.

A topic of prime importance is bullying. In the digital age, it is easier than ever for students to bully, especially cyberbullying. This phenomenon can be addressed by developing a *Bullying Investigation Committee (B.I.C.)*. The committee is comprised of the principal or assistant principal, counselor, media specialist, physical education teacher, and at least one more teacher who is familiar with the student body. The term *bullying* has become pervasive, which places the school in a precarious predicament. Often, parents do not understand the actions that constitute bullying. Therefore, they believe that anything that is said or done falls into this category. It is imperative that the counselor and principal provide parent training designated to understanding the characteristics of bullying. Although an action may be inappropriate, it does not necessarily mean that it is bullying.

Bullying is defined as an individual or group of individuals who use their power to intimidate, harass, or harm another. Typically, this is done in a continuous and systematic manner. The term also references dynamics that are set up to intentionally isolate a student in the school setting. Principals walk a fine line when making determinations of bullying. It is a worthwhile endeavor to get out front of this issue.

The Bullying Investigation Committee is a great defense. The committee interviews all parties involved, potential witnesses, and the classroom teacher. The information is documented on the *B.I.C.* form, which will include the findings, recommendations, and committee signatures. The counselor or principal informs the parent of the findings. The parent may not agree with the findings, but the evidence is provided that the school acted in good faith by thoroughly investigating the allegations. This information may serve as legal documentation. It is better to err on the side of caution instead of dismissing a complaint as trivial. Students are faced with many adversities with as many origins; unfortunately, the school bears the greatest burden of allegations, sometimes unfairly. Therefore, it is imperative for principals to exercise due diligence when handling delicate situations. *All students have a right to an education, but that right does not supersede the rights of other students.*

Principals must continue to be proactive by developing discipline protocol for their school. They must determine how minor offenses, repeated minor offenses, and more serious student offenses will be handled. This should be explained in the discipline protocol. Typical interventions include a verbal warning, time out in and out of the classroom, and a note and phone call to parents, which should be a part of each teacher's management system. Teachers must be trained to manage student behavior or the administration will be rendered ineffective. Professional development dedicated to dealing with students who are defiant and trauma-sensitive is imperative. Again, the training should highlight triggers that provoke negative behavior. Keeping anecdotal notes make it easier to explain disruptive behavior to parents.

Other steps include a *classroom discipline form* for teachers to send home to parents as a prelude to office referrals. After sending two notices, an *administrative discipline form* is completed. The classroom discipline form is not used in instances of extreme or violent behavior. Teachers must take steps to ensure parents received the forms by keeping a copy and documenting. A follow-up phone call may also be necessary.

Another intervention step is the *Parent Accompany Letter* in which the parent is given the option of spending time in the child's classroom in lieu of a suspension. Doing so enables an observation of the normal routine of the classroom and the necessity of each student to behave. If this option is used, the principal should make sure that the parent has reviewed the *classroom visitation protocol,* which explains that they are there to observe their child only, and there will be no discussion of other students' behavior. The protocol also explains how they are able to interact with their child. If the parent's main concern is the teacher, the principal should participate in the observation to ensure that concerns are addressed fairly. The principal is the authority and the only one charged with evaluating the teacher.

Following established protocol is the key to an orderly environment. When protocol is not followed, teachers become frustrated and sometimes behave in manners that are not in the best interest of the child. Actions such as placing students outside of the classroom unsupervised put the student and teacher at risk. If a student is incorrigible with the full attention of an adult, it can be assumed they will behave worse when left to their own devices. Students left unsupervised may leave the campus or inflict harm to other students, especially those who are younger and more vulnerable. This will be a liability on the teacher and school. The same is true for corporal punishment. Administering corporal punishment puts teachers and principals' careers at risk. There is little to gain by doing so. The principal is responsible for setting the standard for disciplining students by reinforcing expectations and holding teachers accountable for established protocol.

Crowd Control (Assemblies, Events, Legal Guardians)

Fun activities such as assemblies, fall festivals, field days, and field trips can become a logistical nightmare for principals. Procedures must be put in place to monitor this as best as possible. A *pre-planned early dismissal form* completed and signed by office staff prior to the assemblies helps alleviate the onset of a rush and allows office staff to pre-check identification. The parent gives the form to the child's teacher to return to the office after the event.

At this point, the parent is free to take the student for an early dismissal. The form includes the child's name, parent's name, event title, time of dismissal, parent's signature, office staff's signature, and date. It may be helpful to make the form a uniform color so that it is easily identifiable. Parents may be notified of this service in the handbook and school newsletters. *Teachers must remember that no safety net will compensate for getting to know their students' parents and guardians. If they are not familiar with a parent or guardian, they should make an inquiry to the office.*

Outside events such as fall festivals are more difficult to manage. The principal must still put safety measures in place. Parents often walk away with their children without notifying the teacher or signing them out for an early dismissal. This unnecessarily puts the school into panic mode. To discourage parents from this act, an early dismissal table may be set up and manned by a school employee.

Again, parents should be informed of this prior to the event. They must show identification to check the student out of school. There are drawbacks to this strategy since identifications cannot be verified via computer; however, this is better than having no measure at all. A list of names authorized to check students out should be made available by class. At the end of the event, the principal or office staff reads the names of students who received an early dismissal. Teachers are then able to account for students missing in their classroom and act accordingly. Field trips add another dimension to safety issues. Every attempt should be made to acquire chaperones for field trips. A chaperone meeting to discuss procedures and guidelines prior to the trip must be held.

The principal must also deal with other influences that threaten student safety. Each year there are more and more *domestic disputes* between parents. The number of custody issues and court battles are increasing as a result. Therefore, schools must red flag legal decrees that prohibit contact with one or more parents. In some districts, the registering parent serves as the legal guardian and takes precedent over all others unless specified by a court decree. The court decree must say more than visitation or joint custody.

In other words, if there is a dispute over who can have contact with the student (stepmothers, stepfathers, girlfriends, boyfriends, etc.), the registering parent has the final say so. Again, this is determined by district policy. Teachers should be on high alert during assemblies, outdoor activities, etc., and never allow a parent to come to the classroom to get a student for an early dismissal. Exterior doors should remain locked during the day and never propped open for convenience. All visitors should enter the school at one designated location. Many districts have systems set up in which visitors must be buzzed in by office staff. All employees should be reminded to report any visitor without a name tag to the office.

Surveillance (School Cameras)

Maintaining *surveillance* during concerts allows organizers to observe issues regarding safety. Many school systems use technology to help secure campuses and protect them from theft. While principals cannot totally rely on cameras to govern the environment, they can use them to aid in promoting safety. Cameras should be placed in strategic areas throughout the school including high traffic areas such as the office, gym, cafeteria, hallways, entrances, carlines, etc. They may also be used as evidence in discipline cases. However, the principal must be careful not to make this the norm as there are areas where cameras are not allowed, such as student restrooms. Parents cannot be given the impression that the only way to implement the code of conduct is through video footage; this is like believing that DNA evidence is required to prove *all* cases. Additionally, parents should not be allowed to view videos due to the confidentiality of other students. This evidence should only be produced when requested from the school board or subpoenaed.

Investigative skills are still needed to provide due process and enforce the discipline policy. Statements should be taken from victims and witnesses upfront as they tend to change over time. Administrators should record the interview date, name of interviewee, questions asked, and answers given. It is customary to take a random sampling in situations when witnesses are unknown. A file should be kept for future reference. Cameras may be used in more proactive ways, as well. Principals are expected to be in many places at one time. A good way to accomplish this is by placing cameras on full screen to view physical education classes, lunch waves, hallways, and even the carline. This provides a snapshot of the environment. The principal must become one with the security system when in her office. Even while conducting conferences, she should inherently know what is happening in the hallways when others do not.

Directing Traffic (Student Dismissal)

Directing the *flow of traffic* is a massive undertaking during concert events. Organizers must not only ensure ample parking space but control the flow in and out of the event. Principals are responsible for the flow and procedures for student dismissal. This entails gaining an understanding of the multiple modes of transportation and the percentage of students utilizing each. To begin, a *transportation depot* (daycare, carline, buses, walkers, vans, etc.) should be created for every mode, taking into consideration space and scheduling. Who, what, and where should be specified on the dismissal duty schedules.

All parents should complete a *transportation form* that is followed unless changed in writing. Changes made over the phone put students and the school at-risk. *Transportation labels* make this process run smoother. Using packaging tape, the teacher securely wraps the label around the strap of the student's book bag. Labels should be created each year for cars, buses, vans, walkers, afterschool daycare, etc. It is best to use colored pictures to assist young students by including the student's name and picture of transportation mode. The bus and number along with the name of the bus driver should also be included, when applicable. *Dismissal logs* record how each student leaves the custody of the teacher by recording the time or whether the student was absent. Each afternoon, logs are submitted to the principal in case there is a question about students' whereabouts after the teacher has left for the day. *Dismissal tags* for vehicles also make the process run smoother.

Bus safety is an ongoing issue that principals face. *Safety drills* must be conducted in accordance with district policy. While some districts may have additional supervisory personnel to ride buses, many do not. This creates unwanted dynamics of inappropriate behavior for bus drivers to manage. Since their primary responsibility is to transport students to and from school, the principal must intervene by sending a *bus notice* home at the beginning of each year to set expectations. The letter explains bus rules and consequences and requests that all elementary-aged students are accompanied by an adult at the bus stop for safety reasons. The bus notice should be signed and returned to the school to be kept on file for future reference.

Additional bus notices may be sent during the year if inappropriate behavior is chronic. The principal should make sure that she has boarded the bus to discuss consequences with students or met with the whole group in her office. This may also include monitoring the bus stop, hosting a formal parent meeting to share concerns, or reviewing video footage from the bus to issue consequences. All students should be issued a bus notice for parents to sign if problems are pervasive. The parents should be informed of the severity of the problem and the consequences that will follow. Appropriate behavior is a matter of safety and is non-negotiable.

Students who walk home from school pose safety issues, as well. There are elements that are out of the principal's control once students leave school property. Issues such as two families feuding in the community spill over into the school. Whereas this is an issue for parents and the legal system, the principal can serve as a mediator. Getting permission from parents to stagger the release of students creates a separation that may assist with the problem. Parents should also be encouraged to have an adult or older sibling to accompany students.

Pre-Show Run-Through (Safety Drills)

Practicing or doing a *pre-show run-through* for an event makes them run smoother. Like the pre-show run-through, safety drills are essential to getting students used to exercising safety procedures. They also prepare students for unforeseen events; therefore, the faculty calendar includes designated days for drills to not forget. A documentation log is kept in the office with dates, times, drill duration, and comments. Common drills include a fire drill, severe weather drill, and an intruder alert or lockdown drill. The principal is responsible for ensuring that all drills are carried out efficiently.

A *fire drill* is typically conducted once per quarter in which students are trained to exit the building quickly to a pre-determined location. A map outlining the location is posted near the classroom door. Once the signal has sounded, students exit the building as quickly and orderly as possible, as indicated on the map. Students must be taught that in case the signal sounds and they are not with their class, they are to join and stay with a class that is exiting the building. A class roll kept on a clipboard in a designated area of the room makes it quickly retrievable. A three-bell signal is sounded when it is safe to re-enter the building. The fire department will need this information for their records. In addition, the principal must also make sure that all fire extinguishers are up to date.

Severe weather drills should be conducted at least once per semester for weather conditions, including tornadoes and hurricanes. A tornado watch means that conditions are right for a tornado to develop and that thunderstorms and tornadoes are likely. A tornado warning means that a tornado has been detected by radar or spotted by an individual. Students should be trained to take shelter immediately when they notice: twisting, funnel-shaped clouds, large hail, loud roaring noise like a train, strong winds, or damage on the ground.

A tornado may not always be visible. Anyone outside at the time of the signal is instructed to go to the nearest building. If the activity is too far from a building, they should seek shelter in a ditch, culvert, or any spot low to the ground avoiding power lines and telephone poles. Students should report immediately to the designated area described on the emergency exit map and crouch down on their knees facing the wall with their hands on the backs of their heads. This position may be uncomfortable for long periods of time; however, it is believed to offer the best protection should a tornado hit the facility. Students must stay away from doors, windows, and outside walls and protect their heads. In case the signal sounds and they are not with their class, they should not return to their classroom but join and remain with a class that is close by and seeking shelter.

Regrettably, students are being educated in a new era–the age of the school shooter. Therefore, school safety has taken on new meaning. It is necessary that students are prepared for emergencies involving intruders through *lockdown drills*. During practice drills, the announcement must be stated as such to avoid unnecessary panic, such as, *"We are implementing a lockdown drill at this time."* Similarly, a real alert should be announced, *"We are implementing lockdown at this time."* Teachers should instruct students to move quickly and quietly to follow protocol by covering windows and locking the door. It is essential for students to practice being quiet during drills. Practice makes perfect and permanent. Students in the hallway must be trained to enter the nearest teacher's classroom.

Each week should begin by reviewing and discussing procedures along with fire and severe weather drill information. Physical education classes that are inside should line up and move into a secure area such as an equipment room and lock the doors. Classes that are outside when the lockdown drill occurs should practice moving to an alternate safe location. All students should be trained to move in the opposite direction of the threat if it occurs outside. The physical education department should review the drills at the beginning of every month as a part of lesson plans.

Once the threat is over, the all-clear signal should be given by a designated bell sequence. *Positions should be maintained until then.* The teacher needs to check roll to account for all students. Rolls must be continuously updated as new students are assigned. Teachers must remember that no plan is perfect or full-proof. Prudent judgment must be exercised! A threat to a school should always be taken seriously because it is impossible to determine in advance whether the threat is real or the work of a prankster. Should there be a bomb threat, the principal should contact the sheriff's department, school system security, and instruct teachers to lead students immediately from the building, taking their class roster to check attendance. The teacher should inform administration of any student who is not with the class and caution students not to pick up any object, known or unknown.

Personnel selected for a school is crucial to its success. Like the A&R Executive (artist and repertoire) for a record label, principals are talent scouts looking for personnel that will be in harmony with the school's vision and mission. Just as artists may be vastly different (pop, soul, rock, jazz, blues, etc.), employees differ in ability levels, personalities, and preferences. Candidates for hire should match the school's needs. For instance, a talent scout searching for the next great pop artist would not sign an opera singer for this purpose. Likewise, a principal whose school has a pervasive theme of technology should recommend candidates with similar interests and aptitude or at least a willingness and desire to learn. Once teachers are recommended for hire, it becomes the principal's responsibility to ensure their actions are conducive to promoting the school program.

Band Members Traits (Understanding Behaviors)

Band members not only play different instruments but adopt unofficial roles in the organization, such as mediator or leader. This is largely determined by personalities and experiences. Principals get to know their band members through interactions but also by essentially *people watching*. This enables a greater understanding of the staff and how they affect or contribute to the school environment and program. Human traits or characteristics will have an impact on the ultimate success of the school. Employee behaviors can be classified in three categories: *leaders, learners, and distractors.*

Leaders are positive contributors to the school program. Often energetic and innovative, they are identified through their ability to effectively perform their job and their zest to develop professionally. Their duties are completed thoroughly and timely, usually going beyond what is required. Leaders are often reluctant to be identified as such for fear of how co-workers will perceive them. However, they are a significant part of the foundation in all successful school programs.

Learners have not reached their optimal level of performance but show great promise if provided systematic support. New teachers and those interested in growing professionally are generally included in this category. Learners are characterized by their ability to accept constructive criticism and put suggestions and new knowledge into action. By doing so, they become a productive part of the school team. Learners must be inundated, but not overwhelmed, with professional development opportunities, as they are future leaders.

Distractors are negative leaders who distract from the school program. They may come in many forms. As in a multiple-choice answer, a distractor may be easy or difficult to identify. While some behaviors are obvious, others may seem more plausible. Overt behavior such as failure to perform professional responsibilities, frequent absences, inappropriate behavior towards students and peers, and insubordinate behavior is fairly easy to recognize. However, covert activities such as undermining the school program through duplicitous means while giving the illusion of being a team player is more difficult to detect. Distractors are normally somewhat gifted in psychology. They attempt to study those around them to identify their Achilles heel and then capitalize during opportune moments.

Therefore, it is imperative for the principal to utilize human relation skills to promote buy-in. This may be accomplished by increasing involvement in leadership decision-making. Providing a voice sometimes reduces dissent. The principal must know how to strategically plan to lessen this employee's negative impact on co-workers and the school program through actions such as creative scheduling and assignments. However, the main focus should not be on the distractor, but on those who promote the program.

Employee Behaviors

Leaders	Learners	Distractors
Positive leadership skills	Developing leadership skills	Negative leadership skills
Team-oriented	Team-oriented	Ego-centric
Subject-matter experts	Novice level instruction	Skilled or unskilled in subject-matter
Leads professional learning	Engages in professional learning	Rejects professional learning

Innovative practices	Open to new ideas	Resistant to change
High student achievement	Inconsistent student achievement	High or low student achievement
Promotes school program	Supports school program	Undermines school program
Requests constructive criticism	Accepts constructive criticism	Rejects constructive criticism

Band Rules (Attendance and Progressive Discipline)

One of the most important rules of the band is for the member to make rehearsals and performance dates, as well as follow a set of established norms. Employees need to attend work unless unavoidable circumstances prevent them from doing so. The way the principal handles absences can have a positive or negative impact on attendance. Therefore, it is imperative to model a good work ethic and lead by example. Expectations should be discussed upfront, which includes contacting the principal personally when absent and using a reporting system to ensure that adequate supervision is provided for students. Reporting absences by email or text is not sufficient, as technology can be unreliable.

Band rules also outline other acceptable behaviors. Depending on the school's culture and make-up, principals can find themselves spending more time managing people than focusing on the role of the instructional leader. It is important to be an instructional leader first and a manager second. The principal must know the difference and understand that employees who do not choose to be willing participants in their development will not make improvements. The progressive discipline process addresses those experiencing problems related to job performance or professionalism. Whether it is attendance or time off task, it is best to begin with a verbal warning. This avoids the perception of disciplining employees for small isolated infractions. However, small infractions can quickly spiral into behavior patterns. Therefore, it is best to record the verbal warning on a calendar or in the note section of a phone for future reference.

Future infractions are noted on a simple *Today I Observed* form. It includes the employee's name, date, brief description of the infraction, and the principal's signature. The *Today I observed* form is a reminder that improvement is needed before formal actions are taken. It gives the employee an opportunity to correct the issues. After a few (2 to 3) are gathered, future communications are placed on formal school letterhead and succinctly written with cumulative details of ongoing issues. Immediate corrective actions are outlined, along with consequences should actions not be taken. Obtaining the employee's signature of receipt provides documentation of the intervention and steps taken for improvement.

When behavior(s) persists, it is time to develop an individual improvement plan. Improvement plans may be used to address issues such as instructional delivery, attendance, time on task, insubordination, workplace harassment, failure to supervise students, lesson plans, etc. Providing literature related to the infraction may help the employee understand the issue better. Due to the nature and sensitivity of employee relations, strong human relationship skills are necessary to successfully implement the strategy. The school culture must support a continuous growth model. The difference will be one of receptivity rather than resistance. Areas in need of improvement must be clearly stated, being careful not to select too many areas at one time.

The employee is given a letter detailing the purpose, actions and activities to be undertaken, and the due date for completion. Activities may include reading related literature and writing a reflection and plan for improvement. The plan may also include meeting with the principal weekly to review the class's proficiency rate, providing a synopsis of weekly parent conferences held, attending a training on classroom management, developing a classroom management system, or undergoing side-by-side coaching. The employee and principal sign the individual improvement plan and hold follow-up meetings as needed. In rare occasions, a grade level change may remedy some problems. When all strategies, within reason, have been exhausted or the employee fails to put forth the effort to improve, a referral to the human resource division of the school district is the next step. Detailed written documentation will be necessary if this step is taken.

Assessing the Performance (Summative Evaluations)

Performance evaluations that include constructive criticism help the artist or teacher to improve their craft. However, to evaluate an employee is to render a judgment which is never easy. This is compounded by the fact that most evaluations are summative and do not provide an opportunity for immediate improvement. Common areas of disagreement are attendance, effective delivery of instruction, the performance of professional duties, professional behavior, and professional dress. In some instances, the employee may not have a clear understanding of why an indicator may be rated lower, which becomes an area of contention. In this case, knowledge is power. The principal should discuss expectations for performance upfront.

In addition, counseling sessions held during the year will provide insight into the employee's progress. A copy of the summative evaluation from the previous year may be used during the sessions. It may not be necessary to score every indicator, assuming all other areas are ranked satisfactorily. The same working document should be used throughout the year, updating it as needed. Encouraging employees to provide concrete evidence during counseling sessions promotes self-evaluation and ensures they receive credit for their actions.

Artistic Differences (Workplace Conflict, Privacy)

It is common for artists or employees to have differences in opinions, especially when they are passionate about their craft. However, disagreements must be handled with a high degree of decorum. When employees have workplace conflict, school-wide professional development in conflict resolution must be provided. To address specific conflicts, the principal must meet with all parties concerned. Norms for the meeting should be established including each party listening intently without interruption and speaking to the principal rather than each other. The principal should urge the employees to state the facts in the simplest terms possible. This reduces the temptation to relive the incidents and escalate tempers. In some situations, there is clearly a right and a wrong. In most situations, there are actions from both parties that lead to the conflict. The principal must outline each and discuss alternative solutions. Employees must be reminded that the expectation of professionalism is not voluntary but a contractual obligation. If students are expected to behave in an acceptable manner, then the burden is even greater for adults. A verbal and written decision should be rendered. If the problem persists, a referral to human resources is necessary.

Principals must also address how faculty and staff use cell phones and recording devices in the school. While most employees have access to cell phones, providing guidelines for acceptable use on school property is still needed. This includes directions for using phones during instruction, duty assignments, professional development, meetings, etc. Specific guidelines should be given for audio or video recording of colleagues and students according to board policy and state law. Some states allow recording as long as one party is privy to the conversation that is being recorded; however, that does not include recording information from a third party. When secretly recording, there is no way to delineate peripheral conversations such as in the hallway, front office, etc. Other states do not allow recording of conversations unless consent is obtained from all parties. Most laws were written to allow conversations to be recorded as a matter of record and not to promote general espionage behavior, as this makes for an uncomfortable school environment. Using cellphones to take pictures of students who misbehave should also be prohibited due to the disturbance caused to parents and concerns of how the image may be used on social media.

School personnel is very important to the success of its students. The art of staffing a school is an enormous task. Finding the right personnel to carry out the vision of the school can be challenging; therefore, it is incumbent upon principals to be purposeful in the quest for employees. A new principal will have the task of helping to align its personnel with the school's vision. Based on the needs of the students, this takes time and skill. Therefore, a plan must be developed for building the faculty that fits the school's needs and its students. Plans such as this work better when a team is created to ensure buy-in from the already existing staff and perhaps parents as well. Effective team building is a collaborative effort.

Chapter Nine

<u>Shining Star</u>

Building Leadership Capacity

There are various levels of expertise to producing a platinum album. The team that creates and promotes music is just as important as the song itself. A flaw at any step can result in a flop rather than a top ten hit. While the principal is the frontman who delivers the song and performance to the public, no one person possesses the level of expertise and commitment needed to run an effective school program; therefore, the principal must build capacity.

Capacity building is the process by which schools improve and retain the skills, knowledge, and resources needed to do their jobs competently. It allows individuals and organizations to perform at a greater magnitude, especially if they can develop others to help with leadership opportunities. Principals need to remember although they are leaders of a school, they are teachers of teachers. Teachers need to be aware of the high expectations of developing leaders from within the building. The first year in the school may not afford the opportunity to acquire the team that is needed to reach the school's full potential. Therefore, it is very important to be goal-oriented and explicit in expectations.

A Star is Born (Developing Teacher Leaders)

Within the walls of each school is a collection of rare finds much like finding a collection of songs written by some of the greatest artists of all times (The Beatles, Whitney Houston, Rolling Stones, Prince, etc.). Although the songs have never been produced, their potential value is astronomical. In the same way, there are superstars in every school with invaluable potential who are ready to shine. With the proper guidance, the principal can encourage the next generation of leaders. There are *five principles* necessary to build capacity or develop *S.T.A.R.S.* in a school.

Principals must keep in mind that every employee has star potential; therefore, their ultimate job is to extract the star quality. The first step is to **survey** the staff to determine training, skills, and interests. This may be conducted through several mediums, which include discussions and written or electronic surveys. A comprehensive list of training and interests may also be used to identify areas of high aptitude. A teacher who needs support in teaching reading may be a whiz with technology.

At the same time, another may have great human relation skills, possess a strong math or science background, may be artistically inclined, or a great public speaker. The skills and talents can be combined to enhance the school program. Hobbies and interests can also be utilized for instruction and extracurricular activities such as sports, drama, music, and dance. Once the staff is surveyed, the principal will need to provide **training** in order to enhance the employee's skill set, especially in core subject areas, mandated initiatives, and the use of technology.

Although teachers may not be gifted in the same areas, there are responsibilities they must all perform at a level of competence; therefore, professional development is a crucial stage in this process. Better training promotes better instruction which promotes better student achievement. Professional development should address instructional needs but also be geared towards interest. Beyond training, principals must *acknowledge* the employee's talent by including them on various committees and decision-making processes. It also means acknowledging the importance of their work before peers, parents, and the community. This can be accomplished through announcements on the intercom, faculty meetings, data meetings, professional development, school assemblies, social media, certificates, awards, trophies, or written in the school newsletter. It is imperative to find opportunities to celebrate employees. When employees see themselves as a vital part of the school program, they begin to take on more ownership, thereby increasing confidence and competence.

The next step is to help teachers *refine* their knowledge so that it may be maximized in the school program. Not every idea will be showroom ready and may need to be tweaked to be feasible and/or effective. Again, the culture of the school will vastly affect the process. The culture must be one of openness and collaboration. Often, teachers have been trained in specific programs that may not be holistic in nature, such as phonics, etc. This may require additional training to provide a balanced literacy approach or advance training beyond their initial training to ensure more effective instruction. The principal can be instrumental in this process through observations, feedback, and setting up learning opportunities.

Lastly, leadership capacity has to be **sustained.** This effort must be systematic and continuous. An effective principal cannot lose sight of the importance of creating leaders in the school by building a cadre of successors to replace leaders as they advance through their career or those who take an extended leave of absence. Therefore, each leader in the school should have a second-in-command to fulfill their duties. This includes administrators, committee chairpersons, testing coordinators, etc. *STARS*, which includes subject-specific experts, should be designated for every school program area, including reading, math, science, social studies, writing, technology, counseling, parenting, etc. Once *STARS* are assigned, they are responsible for keeping abreast of changes at the local, state, and federal levels and leading professional development for other staff. The principal is instrumental in this process by hosting frequent leadership team meetings to determine the next steps.

Choreographers (Utilizing the Experts)

Schools utilize experts or choreographers such as reading and math coaches to assist with learning new steps of programs and initiatives. Their specific knowledge beyond the classroom makes them an asset to the school program. They are particularly helpful in assisting new teachers with instructional practices that are unique to the school. Subject-specific coaches help with strategies in respective areas of the school program through multileveled jobs providing instruction, modeling, side-by side coaching, mentoring for teachers, and working beside the principal to analyze data. They provide follow-up after the principal has identified certain instructional gaps in student achievement. The math and reading coaches are not evaluators, but they are beneficial to teacher development. They can make the difference in the instructional atmosphere of a school.

Counselors and media specialists are also very important figures in an effort to build capacity in a school. The counselor needs to be hands-on with student programs such as the large and small group counseling sessions, career education, community involvement, honor society, and parent programs. They are also at the center of testing by emphasizing test-taking skills, providing teachers with the guidelines, and setting up the testing atmosphere for local and state testing. The media specialist's primary job is to motivate students to become life-long readers by getting them excited about reading books. Among many responsibilities is storytelling time for students in the primary grades and teaching students about technology, library and research skills, and genres.

Communication is important between the principal, teachers, and staff. Therefore, having a good grade-level leader helps with conveying pertinent information from the principal. Teachers are more apt to communicate openly with their peers than with administrators. If they need clarification, they feel less apprehensive about asking their peers. Therefore, grade-level chairpersons are essential for relating to colleagues. They need to be good communicators, knowledgeable, and willing to help. Like other professions, collaboration has taken the forefront of most careers. Education is no different, which poses the argument that true self-contained classrooms are a thing of the past. The era of teachers making the ultimate decision about student achievement is over. Schools now must adhere to accountability. Thus, the grade the school gets from the state report card is everyone's grade and not just the teacher's or class's.

Chapter Ten

Computer Love

Technology

Music continuously evolves as listener preferences change. Over time, styles have vastly transformed from archaic genres such as doo-wop and crooning to more modern genres like rap and pop. Technology devices for listening have followed a similar trend. Once upon a time, the record player, 8 Track, Boom Box, and CD player were all considered the latest technology for listening to music, only to be replaced by more functional outlets such as Sirius, Smartphones, and Alexa. From CDs to BYOD and drones to robots, instruction in schools continues to evolve. Similarly, schools must continue to evolve technologically so students can compete globally. This compels the principal to ensure that students are instructed today for a workforce of tomorrow by immersing them in the digital world with an assortment of technology tools and strategies. Unlike education in earlier years when desks were bolted to the floor in a straight row and students a captive audience, instruction today must be more integrative and collaborative. Technology bridges this gap through the use of various platforms.

Digital Audio Workstation (Digital Literacy)

Music production requires specialized personnel and equipment. First and foremost, it requires a *digital audio workstation (DAW).* The DAW serves multiple functions, including recording, editing, and creating audio files. The DAW allows the producer to mix and alter multiple tracks in music. Digital literacy professional development allows teachers to select and edit strategies for use in the classroom. Platforms such as Discovery Education provide training and digital tools to enable teachers to deliver authentic technology-based instruction that addresses students' various learning styles. The debate is usually *how* technology should be integrated, not *if*. Technology empowers students to be more creative and more connected by super-charging how they learn today.

Musical Instrument Digital Interface (One -to-One Devices)

The second most essential music production equipment is the *musical instrument digital interface (MIDI)*. The MIDI is a grid controller which is similar to a keyboard. It controls beats and allows producers to arrange and sequence music. Teachers can apply this concept in schools that have one-to-one devices such as laptops and electronic tablets. Interfacing with students is accomplished by setting up learning boards so students may complete online instructional activities as designated by the teacher. The most effective online instructional practices include reports that can be reviewed and discussed with students to determine growth. By doing so, learning is intentional. Hosting data talks or student conferences help to optimize achievement. Interfacing with students also includes using one-to-one devices to check for understanding.

Delivery of instruction is only as successful as a student's ability to understand. Using computer tools to check for understanding allow teachers to know exactly which students have mastered a concept and which ones have not. As students answer on individual computers, their choices populate the interactive board. Other tools let teachers randomly select students to answer specific questions, keeping everyone on task.

One-to-one devices also relieve a lot of stress placed on schools when completing mandatory online assessments. Schools that are equipped can practice daily while others must maneuver within one or two labs. It should be noted that there is a big difference in paper-pencil assessments and those that require students to manipulate tools and navigate back and forward to answer questions. One-to-one devices allow this type of practice as students work on reading passages, solving mathematical tasks, and completing open-ended questions or writing tasks. Students who do not have common access are placed at a disadvantage.

Studio Headphones (Digital Citizenship)

The third type of equipment that is needed is *studio headphones*. Studio headphones filter unwanted sound and help to maintain audio fidelity so that the consumer gets a clear message. Teaching digital citizenship establishes acceptable use and filters unacceptable behaviors so that students use equipment safely and for the intended purpose. Students' use of technology and digital citizenship go hand in hand. It is the teacher's responsibility to ensure devices are used responsibly. Some school systems engage in BYOD (bring your own device) when there are not enough school-supplied devices for all students to use. Students bring an array of technology tools to school in order to complete instructional tasks. Parents are required to sign a contract with the schools for the students to bring their own devices.

The system places the students' devices on the system network. One of the drawbacks of BYOD is acceptable use, especially cyberbullying. Oftentimes, issues that arise in the community spill over into the school. Schools must develop a strong acceptable use policy that strictly outlines appropriate behavior when using devices. The policy must include consequences for cyberbullying, as well as protect students against internet predators, scammers, and inappropriate social media. The counselor and media specialist should address the aforementioned in digital literacy training for students and teachers.

Audio Interface (Learning Platforms, Broadcasting)

An *audio interface* is different from the MIDI in that it converts music from instruments such as the guitar into a digital format for delivery. There are a variety of audio interfacing that occurs in schools which include converting from traditional instructional methods to alternative methods. Virtual (web-based instruction), remote (not physically on campus), and blended learning (online and face-to-face) have gained traction over the years. *Virtual leaning* is a well-thought-out instructional platform that is primarily conducted online with virtual interactions with the teacher. Students follow a syllabus and are able to pace instruction according to time and need. When students are unable to attend school, they can engage in instructional activities with the teacher through *remote learning*. This is accomplished through video conferencing using several mediums. *Blended learning* is a mixture of online learning and face-to-face learning.

The key to each method of instruction is planning, organization, and communication. Teachers must plan instruction based on standards that will be taught and the materials that will be used to support instruction. Planning is followed by the careful organization of assignments and resources that can be easily navigated by students. Too many files and folders can become overwhelming for students which affects their ability to complete assignments. It is also essential to provide methods of two-way communications within the platform, as well as email, phone, written, and face-to-face when possible. Status letters that inform parents of their child's current level of performance and missed assignments may be necessary when students are in danger of failing. Consistent communication addresses the greatest challenges associated with virtual, remote, and blended learning: the lack of systematic face-to-face interactions. Although students are given autonomy, educators must not forget their role in providing support, guidance, and building good study habits.

Other interfacing methods include interactive boards, broadcasting, DMS's, and collaboration labs. Grade-level collaborative daily lessons taught from interactive boards allow systematic navigating through subjects and concepts in a cohesive manner. This gives students on grade level an opportunity to get the same level of instruction. Interactive boards can also be used to build background knowledge, especially for vocabulary in nonfiction text. This is important when students are reading about complex and unfamiliar topics. Vocabulary activities aid comprehension by matching words to images to help students understand concepts during whole group and small group instruction. The use of technology for teachers makes their jobs a lot easier by working collaboratively on plans at specific grade levels. Thematic units can be edited by multiple teachers. This makes teamwork more effective because everything is connected.

Engaging in daily or weekly broadcast programs led by student anchors is the most common method for students to deliver the morning announcements, pledge of allegiance, and thought for the day. Weekly broadcast programs can be enjoyable to students and parents by providing up-to-date news and reminders about school events. Broadcast programs offer students the opportunity to learn new technologies and the varied career roles that go into producing. It is a good way to get students interested in television production and the ever-evolving realm of technology. A successful broadcasting program requires green room equipment such as special lighting, video cameras, speaker systems, and laptops.

Digital Monitoring Screens (DMS) placed throughout the school help students learn prerequisite skills such as basic facts, high-frequency words, and vocabulary. Placing the DMS in hallways, cafeteria, classrooms, and over water fountains give students constant reinforcement of concepts. In addition, the DMS offers subliminal learning during non-instructional time by helping students with vocabulary and math instruction, etc. Teachers may also upload instructional videos as part of center activities while small groups are conducted.

Collaboration Labs or *Computer Café's* provide a place for students to complete research projects. Developing the spaces take time and finances; however, they increase students' learning opportunities. Students need to begin to prepare for the world of work as early as elementary school. The labs provide a simulation of future workforces where students develop soft skills when working and collaborating with others. Also, they allow engagement in problem-solving tasks, which are skills needed to be successful in chosen careers. The labs also lend themselves to project-based learning in which students conduct research in a variety of subjects including science and social studies

The Showcase (Technology Night)

Artists showcase their talent to gain a following. Hosting a technology showcase builds a closer relationship between parents and the school. This is not a time to talk about technology but to immerse parents in how it is used in the school program through activities such as friendly competitions using the interactive boards, coding drones, or watching short performances and presentations from students via movie clips. In conjunction with how technology is used, schools must help parents understand and utilize other resources such as free district resources, online platforms, programs for registering or grading, parent-teacher communications, common sites used for recreational reading, eBooks owned by the school, tutorial support for reading and math, etc. A list of websites used by the school will provide parents with the necessary resources to assist their child at home.

Technologically Challenged (Technical Difficulties)

For all of the advantages technology affords, it is not without challenges. Along with a fear of inappropriate use is the teacher's level of confidence and the fear of proper functioning during instruction. Operational equipment is a must, whether it is a singing performance or teaching performance. Districts must provide the infrastructure to support and manage technology devices. Among other things, this includes firewalls for protection and servers that are functional. Many online programs and assessments will require students to access the internet simultaneously; therefore, servers must have the capability to handle the mass usage.

Meanwhile, districts have to filter unauthorized content while protecting a massive amount of confidential data in schools. Funding technology can also be challenging for some schools. Most states will provide limited funding for this endeavor. Schools with federal programs such as Title I get some assistance. However, schools that do not qualify, struggle to keep up with technology trends. They usually must find grants, fundraise, and tap into public officials' discretionary funds to get enough funds to update their technology.

Principals must take a leap of confidence when it comes to communicating to teachers and sharing information using technology by modeling during presentations. Technology is here to stay; hence, leaders must learn to utilize it and support teachers and students in its use.

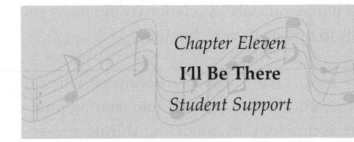

Music evokes a range of emotions in the average listener. It can be reminiscent of lost or unrequited love or evoke memories of happier times. Most people have at least one special song that affects the psyche in a positive way. It is part of their coping mechanism. Music has served in many capacities, including being taught as a subject, as a calming mechanism while students work, to teach skills and concepts, transition students, and promote rhythm and movement. The objective is for the song or music to fit the needs of the students. Likewise, the principal's playlist must include a comprehensive support system to help students cope with barriers to achievement. This begins with creating an environment that uplifts and motivates students to be the very best version of themselves. Teaching is as much a labor of love as it is the art of pedagogy. There is no instructional method or mathematical equation that supports, motivates, and builds self-esteem like an educator.

Music Therapy (Removing Barriers to Achievement)

The music therapy health professional uses music to tap into clients' emotions, thereby enabling communication. Barriers that impede the experience of a full life are unlocked through this process. Successful schools take deliberate actions to promote a positive *social and emotional environment* to remove barriers to achievement. More than ever before, schools and education are in crisis. The nostalgia of yesteryears when soda pop and sock hops reign supreme is long gone. Teaching has become a complex career fraught with daily challenges. Students are entering schools with a legion of social and emotional issues that require extra support from teachers, such as exemplified in the book *More Than a Bird* by Liz Huntley. The book gives voice to the critical role that educators play in the lives of at-risk students. Supporting students does not end with the teacher, but should involve all employees including cafeteria staff, custodians, and instructional aides who interact with students. Educators must take an affirmative stand when fighting against influences that negatively impact students' learning.

Not all barriers to achievement come from students themselves. Some are a matter of catastrophic events, which include pandemics, floods, tornadoes, hurricanes, and fires. Pandemics such as COVID-19 of 2020 changed the landscape of the world and require schools to rethink how they educated students. A virtual nation under siege, privileges that are usually taken for granted became a luxury when access to food and healthcare are limited, jobs lost, businesses closed, all forms of recreation and socialization halted, and education interrupted.

Students, parents, and staff experienced anxiety when the regular school routine was disrupted. This anxiety was compounded by the unknown. When such events happen, principals must contend with the emotional and academic repercussions. Proactive steps to maintain normalcy must be taken. This process should begin by updating stakeholders with information such as methods of communication, nutritional assistance, educational platforms that will be used for instruction, expectations for students and parents, and status of school-related events.

As with any great leader, the principal must communicate calmly and reassuringly to help all concerned persevere through the crisis. It is said that "necessity is the mother of invention." The COVID-19 pandemic has made the development of a contingency plan for catastrophic events a necessity. This should include a variety of alternate schedules. Just as schools have prepared for fire and severe weather drills, they must now prepare students and parents for remote learning. Therefore, acquiring one-to-one devices must be a priority. When students are required to learn from home, careful consideration must be given to flexible scheduling for those who share devices, as well as those who have multiple teachers. Educators who share students must be sensitive in their expectations and workload assignment. The plan must also allow time for teachers who are also parents to assist their children.

Further, the pandemic compels each school or district to adopt an online platform or method of systematic instruction. Practicing live video conferencing lessons as a regular part of the school program and allowing parents to observe classes at least once per week will make transitioning much easier in the event of an emergency. Principals may take this opportunity to observe lessons electronically, as well. Video conferencing also has positive implications for activities such as IEP meetings, absentee students, faculty meetings, professional development, parent-teacher meetings, parent-principal meetings, district principal meetings, grade-level meetings, parental involvement day, etc.

Career Development (Finding Your Voice)

Knowing where their greatest talent lies is a struggle for many artists. Students have similar experiences when deciding on a career path. It is the school's responsibility to narrow the gap between the abstract and reality through career fairs, speakers, and online career programs. Teachers can also promote career development in their classroom by introducing and discussing various career paths, traditional and non-traditional. During the discussion, it is imperative that teachers dispel gender bias misconceptions as related to careers. Throughout the year, students may be given a list of careers to research and determine what skills are needed such as math, science, or writing; which universities offer the program; how many years of schooling is needed; what is the salary range; and what type of soft skills are needed. By taking these initial steps, students begin to understand career development.

Benefit Concerts (21ˢᵗ CCLC Clubs)

Students not only need help coping with day-to-day issues, but they also need financial support, as well. The 21ˢᵗ CCLC afterschool grant is a significant fund source for this purpose. The grant provides opportunities to help broaden the horizons of students in schools with the greatest needs. By doing so, it opens a world of possibilities that would not otherwise be available. The clubs are free of charge and offer a host of afterschool activities for students while providing needed supervision for working parents. The grant requires that clubs address reading and math, health and nutrition, attendance, behavior, STEM, and the arts through enrichment activities that pique the interests of students. The following are examples of clubs for each component of the grant.

- *Book Cooks* (K-2) is a reading and math club in which literature is brought to life by using skills such as listening, following directions, measurement, counting, sorting, etc., followed by preparing food items to highlight various stories. Students engage in higher-order thinking by making, confirming, and revising predictions, as well as comparing and contrasting stories.
- The *M.A.R.B.L.E. Club – 3-5 (Math and Reading Based on Life Experiences)* focuses on using math-based literature and real-life artifacts to help students build conceptual understanding.
- *Biking for Better Bodies (3-B Club)*, *Step to It*, tennis, archery, and basketball clubs promote health and fitness.
- *Coding, Broadcasting, Engaging Youth in Engineering (E.Y.E.)*, and *SECME* clubs reinforce the STEM component of the grant.
- Clubs dedicated to the Arts include the *Classical Arts and Crafts* club which introduce students to

classical music as they create arts and crafts projects, *Music is Instrumental* in which students create and play an array of DIY instruments, and *Music is the Key* where students learn to play the keyboard and guitar.

All clubs are grade-level sensitive and may be taught by in-house staff or vendors.

Educational excursions also place a financial burden on families. *Field trip fundraisers* help offset the cost of field trips and make them more affordable for students. This can be done by scheduling weekly fundraisers by grade levels. The grade level is responsible for deciding which items to sell, creating order forms, and receipting money. PTO or PTA can assist with purchasing the items. All proceeds go into an account to be used to lower the expense per child, pay for transportation, and pay for indigent students to attend.

Principals should become familiar with other entities that offer services to assist students. They include but are not limited to, those offered by organizations such as Big Brother and Big Sister, food pantry organizations, teen centers, mental health facilities, homeless shelters, and more. Some working parents will need assistance during the morning hours, such as a before school daycare which is typically more cost-effective than community daycare services. However, schools still need to compile a list of community daycares for parents' convenience.

Personal Assistants (District Support)

Personal assistants accompany and assist artists as needed, much like the ongoing assistance from the school district that is provided to schools. The student services division provides a wide range of services such as health training, transportation for students, uniforms, assistance for the homeless, registration, and discipline to name a few. They also conduct required health training for employees and screenings for students. Some schools are fortunate to have a registered nurse on staff to assist students with serious health concerns. If this is not the case, it will be the responsibility of the principal to set up a system to assist with responsibilities such as administering medicine and attending to students who have accidents.

The employee hired to conduct these duties must understand the need for documentation such as keeping a log of the time medication is administered, the nature and treatment for accidents, and notification of parents. If funds are not available, the principal may create an *Illness Notification Form* in which teachers are required to document pertinent information regarding student's health needs. The illness form should include the nature of the illness, contact number, name of person contacted, and results of the conversation. In accordance with school board policy, the principal should make the ultimate decision if a parent is required to pick a child up from school.

The special education division provides technical support to ensure compliance with regulations. The do's and don'ts can become complicated when dealing with special needs students. This is not an area where the principal should guess. Instead, she must rely on this special service. *A fundamental rule of thumb is students with special needs have the same rights as all others, if not more.* When in doubt, ask. A file with phone numbers for all district divisions and community resources should be readily available.

Education is the springboard to propel students to their destiny. Removing barriers to achievement places students on a trajectory to be successful members of society.

"Education...beyond all other devices of human origin, is a great equalizer of conditions of men --the balance wheel of the social machinery...It does better than to disarm the poor of their hostility toward the rich; it prevents being poor."

Horace Mann

Chapter Twelve
<u>Ain't Too Proud to Beg</u>
School Finance

Music promotion is an elaborate and expensive process. An exorbitant amount of money is invested in preparing the artist and the product. To the public, a popular artist may give the illusion of free-flowing cash, while behind the scenes, there are a magnitude of obligations that must be met before being compensated. Although the artist may be the biggest star, they may not necessarily receive the greatest pay. Comparably, schools are non-profit organizations that receive a limited amount of operational funds. In most schools, the needs greatly outweigh the resources. Consequently, principals must seek funding from a variety of sources. As a chief financial officers of their schools, it is their duty not only to secure funds but also to allocate and monitor the school program's expenditures.

The Bottom Line (Monitoring Expenses)

Record companies keep abreast of the bottom line by monitoring expenditures. This includes money that is allocated to promote the artist such as advertising, traveling expenses, booking venues, wardrobe, video and record production, and sales, etc. The close monitoring process is necessary to track expenses, but also helps to determine profit. Principals engage in this extensive process which begins with following state and district guidelines and being aware of funding sources and their uses. This training is generally provided by the local school accounting department. It is important that the principal has a comprehensive understanding of accounting procedures.

Along with adhering to local school accounting procedures, there are other factors that should be taken into consideration. To start, the principal should be the only one listed on the bank account, sign school checks, or receives the bank statement. Although it may be convenient to do otherwise, it is a risky practice. The checks and balance system provides an opportunity to review processed checks and reconcile the bank statement in accordance to accounting guidelines. Money is a meticulous matter; therefore, each account and transaction must be scrutinized. The principal must also cultivate a good relationship with the bookkeeper in which the process for payroll, invoices, expenditure reports, attendance, purchases, etc., is developed. Normally, a specified day of the week is set aside for this purpose. This practice will ensure that duties and responsibilities are carried out in a timely manner. In-service need to be provided for teachers so there is a systematic process for receipting money, documenting attendance, purchasing materials and supplies, and reimbursing teachers for items purchased.

Reading the Contracts (Earmarked Funds)

Often, money is *earmarked* for certain activities, which means that there are strict guidelines of how the funds can be spent. Stipulations for earmarked funds are non-negotiable and must be followed with fidelity. Artists also have conditions in their contracts such as how much they will be paid and if they are allowed to make music with another company. To avoid legal ramifications, they must read the fine print of their contracts, just as principals must be careful to read the fine print for the appropriate use of various fund sources. An in-depth understanding will allow the maximization of funds to meet the academic needs of students.

The first is *Title I* which originated as part of the *Elementary and Secondary Education Act* of 1965 *(ESEA)*. The primary goal of *Title I* is to *"Improve the Academic Achievement of the Disadvantaged."* Funding is issued based on the school's poverty level using a set formula. It ensures that students who qualify receive equity in funding to enrich instruction. Title I funds can be used for teaching materials, tutoring, technology, parenting, and paying the salaries or stipends of additional personnel who support students in becoming successful. This must be accomplished by supplementing, not supplanting (replacing), resources that are already in existence.

For instance, if a school system purchases a reading or math textbook series, Title I funds cannot be used to supplant or replace funding that is already in place. However, workbooks that are not a part of the contract may be purchased to promote comprehension or increase problem-solving. Schools with a low level of poverty may also qualify for funds through *Title I Targeted Assistance.*

This means that funds are allocated for a specific targeted group of students at the poverty level. In this case, materials and resources may only be used with those students instead of school-wide.

In accordance with the Every Student Succeed Act (ESSA), *Title I* is composed of six parts: *Title I Part A* – Improving Basic Programs Operated by Local Education Agencies, *Title I Part B* – State Assessment Grants, *Title I Part C* – Education of Migratory Children, *Title I Part D* – Prevention and Intervention Programs for Children and Youth Who Are Neglected, Delinquent, or At-Risk, *Title I Part E* – Flexibility for Equitable Per-Pupil Funding, and *Title I Part F* – General Provisions.

The purpose for *Title II* funding is *"Preparing, Training, and Recruiting High-Quality Teachers, Principals, and Other School Leaders"* thereby, improving the instructional program for disadvantaged students. There is a broad range in which this can be accomplished; however, educators must be abreast of the strict criteria for allowable use. The use of funds may include hiring academic coaches, mentoring, stipends for professional development, class size reduction, contracted services, signing bonuses, administrative and support staff salaries (Title II related only), materials and supplies (for professional development only), registration, and travel for conferences. The qualifications for receiving the funds is much like Title I. Title II consists of three parts: *Title II Part A* – Supporting Effective Instruction, *Title II Part B* – National Activities, and *Title II Part C* – General Provisions. Schools may apply for funds through the federal programs division.

The purpose of *Title III* is to provide *"Language Instruction for English Learners and Immigrant Students."* It is also designed to "help ensure that English learners attain English language proficiency and meet state academic standards." It is comprised of two parts: *Title III Part A* – English Language Acquisition, Language Enhancement an Academic Achievement Act and *Title III Part B* – General Provisions. Funding is based on the number of migrant and ELL students, according to the censor report. It is used to provide additional academic assistance to ensure student success. The grant is also used to purchase technology and programs to be used with qualifying students, parent activities of ELL students, as well as teaching material and professional development for ELL or Migrant teachers. The focus on Title III was strengthened by *Every Student Succeed Act (ESSA)"*.

Title IV provides a comprehensive framework that supports *"21st Century Schools"* for students and families. It is comprised of six parts: *Title IV, Part A* - Student Support and Academic Enrichment Grants, *Title IV, Part B* - 21st CCLC Grants, *Title IV, Part C*- Charter Schools, *Title IV, Part D* - Magnet Schools, *Title IV, Part E* – Family Engagement in Education, and *Title IV, Part F* – National Activities. Other ESSA provisions, perhaps lesser-known, include: *Title V – Flexibility and Accountability,* which include *Title V, Part A* – Funding Transferability for State and Local Educational Agencies, *Title V Part B* – Rural Education, and *Title V Part C – General Provisions: Title VI - Indian, Native Hawaiian, and Alaska Native Education, Parts A, B, and C, Title VII –Impact Aide, Title VIII*

– General Provisions Part A-G , and Title IX, Education for the Homeless.

IDEA (Individuals with Disabilities Education Act) is funding for school systems for students with disabilities. The students receiving these funds have an IEP or individualized education program. The funds are used to hire teachers, consultants, psychometrists, and secure technology software and materials. IDEA ensures that states provide intervention for individuals with disabilities that are ages 3-21 *(Part B),* as well as assistance for infants and toddlers ages 2-3 with disabilities *(Part C).* The funding is available for all schools.

Alternative Rock (Schools of Choice)

Alternative rock is a deviation from classic or commercial rock. It is characterized by deliberate changes and distortions in guitar tones, sometimes referred to as grunge. The genre began to receive notoriety in the 1990s through groups like *Nirvana.* However, it had been in existence several decades before. Similarly, schools of choice such as magnet and charter schools provide alternatives to the traditional school program. Public funding makes this possible for students with awards made through the U.S. Department of Education and the and the Magnet Schools Assistance Program. Students could apply to be educated in a school that was not necessarily their zoned neighborhood school.

Magnet schools provide a specialized education driven by a theme such as STEM, performing arts, and preparatory traditional. They have been in existence for over 30 years. Magnet schools usually have a random selection process; however, once admitted, students must meet performance criteria to maintain enrollment status in the school. Research indicates students from low social-economic households who attend magnet schools are more likely to finish school.

Charter schools grew out of the *No Child Left Behind Act of 2002* as a solution to underperforming schools. Some educators strongly support charter schools, while others feel that they only distract from public schools. Much of the debate surrounding the schools includes flexibility in curriculum, student selection and retention, staffing, and accountability. Although the schools receive public funds, charter schools basically develop a contract of operation which is approved by the state in which they operate. Laws may vary from state to state. The curriculum of the charter schools is generally more flexible, allowing more administrative autonomy. Any student may attend, but unlike traditional public schools, they are not guaranteed a space. Students in Charter schools do not have organized sports programs. However, like homeschooling, the students can participate in activities or programs in their local school zone.

Private schools are alternative schools that are funded mainly by parents. The reasons for students to attend a private school may vary. Many times, private schools offer smaller class sizes, greater parental involvement, and more resources. Sports and religious reasons are also among the top reason parents choose private schools. Deciding between private and public schools begins with affordability, but it is also a personal choice. Many parents begin making schooling decisions before students are born. They may purchase homes based on the school district and or the private schools in that area.

Rights and Royalties (District or Site-Based Management)

There is often an extensive discussion between music companies and recording artists regarding royalties and rights to music. Traditionally, music companies own the rights to the artists' songs; however, more and more artists are negotiating deals that allow them to maintain the rights. There has been a similar debate in education over the right to administer funds in the school program. In most cases, the district makes decisions about how funds are used in schools (district-based management); however, based on research and interviews with principals in different parts of the country, some local schools make this decision (site-based management).

The funds are allocated yearly to the local school which determines if they will be used to pay for additional personnel, technology, material and supplies or other needs of the school. The main advantage of this method is that the needs of the school can be addressed more effectively. Principals can align funds to resources for instruction. They may also hire personnel to fit the school's needs by hiring staff such as math and reading coaches, technology teachers, nurses, attendance clerks, support personnel, or parenting specialists.

Generating Funds (For the Love of Money)

Before they reach acclaim status, artists must seek other means of income, such as playing small venues or selling music out of their garage or basement. Although schools receive funding from federal, state, and local governments, alternative methods to generate funds must be considered, as well. This process usually begins with traditional fundraisers such as daily snacks, fall festivals, and field day or spring fling. The leadership team and/or PTA must also meet this responsibility through other creative activities that pique students' interests and increase revenue. In addition, extended day programs are very profitable and a great enhancement for schools. Parents who work late need care for their children, which helps to have this service at school. This type of program pays for itself and makes a good profit without charging parents an extraordinary amount of money.

School-generated funds should be aligned with funds received from federal, state, and local governments to sufficiently meet the needs of students. The federal government contributes on average about 8% of funding, leaving a void to be filled through alternative methods, including those received from state and local governments. Schools heavily rely on ad valorem taxes or property taxes to fund public education. The ad valorem value is based on assessed amounts such as property houses, cars, boats, and other valuables. This is where possible inequities of education begin. Low-income areas cannot afford to contribute as much money towards schools in their district; therefore, inequities regarding facilities and special programs become more apparent. The solution to this problem is then left to the local school and its ability to increase revenue by other means.

Clearly, it takes money to manage any school, whether it is public or private. There is a consensus that suggests the more money spent on education, the better the program will be. However, researchers have learned that how money is spent in schools is more important than how much is acquired, proving that teacher quality and resource use are paramount. Schools that directly align their funds to student achievement experience a greater success rate.

Chapter Thirteen

It Takes Two

Engaging Stakeholders

There are dances that may be performed in a group such as modern line dances; those that are better suited for partners such as ballroom dances; and those performed individually such as hip hop. Certain professions are dependent on the performance of the individual; however, the role of the school principal is not one of them. Being the bell of the ball with no other attendees is purposeless. School administration is a symbiotic relationship that depends on the collaborative efforts between the principal and others; therefore, networking is imperative. Soliciting ideas and input from multiple sources enriches the school program.

Line Dance (Stakeholders)

Variations of line dances are centuries old, although the name itself has a more recent origin. Line dances are characterized by a repeated sequence of steps performed by a group. The group, like stakeholders, must synchronize their actions to accomplish a given task. Most significantly, a line dance must have multiple participants or stakeholders. Unlike dances that have come and gone, the line dance has had longevity, arguably because of its gregarious and participatory nature. Successful schools seek the participation of a wide range of stakeholders to enhance the school program, as well.

What is a stakeholder? *Someone that has a vested interest in students and their success.* The chief stakeholders of every school are the parents. People in the community, businesses, governing officials can commit to becoming vital stakeholders or partners in the education of students. Some stakeholder relationships must be developed and/or nurtured. However, it is the job of the principal to create an inclusive environment to complete the educational triangle; home, school, and community working together for the betterment of children. Developing partnerships with community businesses, churches, colleges, and feeder partner schools is a worthy connection for everyone.

The Tango (PTA/PTO)

Parent-teacher organizations are excellent collaboration networks needed to assist the school. This becomes visible to students as they begin to understand how the support of others makes for a cooperative environment. However, learning to navigate and negotiate with organizations is sometimes a precarious undertaking. Similar to performing the tango, administrators oftentimes have to change positions or make abrupt pauses and turns as they interact. This requires the establishment of clear boundaries. Like the tango, the principal may take one of two positions, close or open. The close position is a chest-to-chest embrace with little or no space, while the open position is an embrace in which there is space between the dancers. The position the principal takes will determine how much autonomy and influence the organization should maintain. Again, this is greatly influenced by the culture and climate of the school. The main question is does the organization share a deep commitment to the vision and mission of the school or does it have a separate agenda. If the school vision is a shared one (close embrace), principals may allow greater decision-making power within the school. That is, the organization is instrumental in the accomplishment of goals. However, when decisions are not conducive to the overall school program such as those posing safety issues, disruptive to the school process, or violates school board policy, the principal must limit the amount of decision-making power (open embrace).

Parent Teacher Organizations can work to assist the principal by setting goals to address issues that affect students. They can help secure funds for schools and assist with special projects. Principals should encourage parents to become members of a PTA or PTO. These groups benefit the school by helping the principal develop worthy fun activities to keep the interest of the students throughout the school year. Meetings should include getting input for activities such as the opening of school events, enhancing the school program or facility, fundraisers, classroom volunteers, teacher appreciation, room mothers, etc. As with anything else in education, some schools struggle to get the necessary parental involvement to work collaboratively with the school. Many of the usual duties that some parent groups carry out, teachers are required to perform in other schools due to limited support. Thus, the principal is required to step in and remedy the problem by developing a committee and an organizational plan for events like the fall festival and spring fling.

Philanthropy (Service Learning and Other Partnerships)

Many artists and celebrities engage in philanthropy by serving as benefactors for non-profit organizations through active participation and financial contribution. This altruistic behavior supports the well-being of all mankind. Generally, this behavior is characterized in schools as service-learning. *Service-learning* refers to learning that involves a reciprocal relationship that benefits students as well as others in the community. At the same time, it keeps the goals of the curriculum in mind. The leadership team may investigate potential community issues to be addressed. The school must then prioritize service-learning issues according to the feasibilities of activities such as cost, time, and potential impact. A committee is designated to organize and carry out various tasks as needed.

Altruism also extends to showing appreciation for partners in education for services rendered to the school. Partner Appreciation allows the school to thank partners, as well as share other pertinent information. Partners have invested time and resources into the school; therefore, they want to know how students perform academically. The principal may take this opportunity to share assessment data, attendance, percent of reading goals met, and other school-related information.

Community guests add value to the school program by sharing their expertise from specific fields of employment. Guest speakers may be selected from a range of backgrounds to participate in activities such as career fairs, ceremonies, or honors assemblies. Community support also comes in other shapes and forms such as teen centers, police departments, doctor offices, dentist offices, mental health facilities, local and state leaders, and the district attorney's office. These entities provide invaluable in-kind resources to the school. State and local officials oftentimes have discretionary funds to support the school. The school-community relationship may also be fostered in the following ways: attending holiday lunches, reading to students, assisting with clubs and art projects, and judging essays, science fairs, and oratorical competitions. Many Greek organizations have a founding principle that includes service to mankind which frequently includes working with schools. Partnering with sororities and fraternities is a source of support for tutoring, fall festivals, spring flings, field day activities, and other events. These organizations also provide support for the academic program.

Schools may also develop an alliance with local universities that supply student teachers and tutoring services for students. To ensure effectiveness, an orientation should be held to provide information on attendance procedures, dress code, performance expectations, and interacting with students. Assigning student teachers to highly qualified staff is advantageous in developing effective teachers. This also allows the school to be represented in the most positive light. Sometimes student teachers are assigned based on the cooperating teacher's lack of classroom management skills. Candidates who are in the learning process themselves cannot provide the support needed. The decision may also result in the transference of unwanted habits.

Schools are a subset of a larger society; therefore, it is vital to collaboratively make decisions that will not only affect the school, but the community as well. Parents, businesses, and local community organizations partnerships are an effective way to accomplish this task. The strength of the collective body enriches student achievement.

<u>Sources</u>

Alabama Literacy Act and Alabama State Department of Education, (2021). *Alabama Course of Study English Language Arts Conceptual Framework*

Benjaminson, Peter (1979). *The Story of Motown*, Grove Press

Burgess, Dave (2012). *Teach Like a Pirate*, Dave Burgess Consulting, Incorporated

Capacity (2013), The Glossary of Education Reform, https://www.edglossary.org/capacity/

Character Counts, *Six Pillars of Character*, (2021). https://charactercounts.org/character-counts-overview/six-pillars/

DuFour, Richard and Rebecca, DuFour, Eaker, Robert, Many, Thomas W., Mattos, Mike
(2016). *Learning, By Doing: A handbook for Professional Learning Communities at Work*, Solution Tree Press, (3rd Edition)

Every Student Succeed Act (2021). National Association of Secondary, https://www.nassp.org/a/every-student-succeeds-act-essa-overview/

Every Student Succeed Act (2021). U.S. Department of Education, https://www.ed.gov/essa?src=ft

Fahey, Jo (2012). *Ways to learning Through Inquiry Guiding Children to Deeper Understanding*, International Baccalaureate

Fosnot, Catherine T. (2015). <u>*Constructivism: Theory, Perspectives, and Practice 2nd Edition,*</u> Teachers College Press

Fountas, Irene and Pinnell, Gay Su (1998). <u>*Word Matters: Teaching Phonics and Spelling in the Reading/Writing Classroom,*</u> Heinemann

Friedman, Milton and Friedman, Rose, Free *to Choose (1990). A Personal Statement)*, Mariner Books, Boston, Massachusetts

Fullan, Michael, (2019). *Leading in a Culture of Change,* Second Edition, Jossey-Bass

Gurian, Michael and Ballew, Arlette C. (2003). *Boys and Girls Learn Differently Action Guide for Teachers*, Jossey-Bass, Inc.

Heathfield, Susan, Progressive Discipline in the Workplace, (2021).The Balanced Career, https://www.thebalancecareers.com/what-progressive-discipline

Huntley, Liz (2015). *More Than a Bird*, Salthouse Publishing,

Johnson, Spencer (2009). *Peaks and Valleys*, Atria Books

Johnson, Spencer (1998). *Who Moved My Cheese*, G. P. Putnam's Sons

Kuhn, Thomas, (2012). *The Structure of Scientific Revolution*, University of Chicago Press

Latham, Allison, (2005). *The Oxford dictionary of Musical Terms*, Oxford University Press

Lawrence, Fennelly and Perry, Marianne (2014). *The Handbook for School Safety and Security*, Butterworth and Heinemann

Lockwood, Lewis (2005). *Beethoven: The Music and the Life*, W.W. Norton

Lundin, Stephen C., Paul, Harry, Christensen, John (2002). *Fish*, Hodder & Stoughton

McGinnis, Alan Loy (2016). *Bringing Out the Best in People, McGraw – Hill Education (3rd Edition)*

McLeod, Saul, *Jean Piaget's Theory of Cognitive Development*, (Retrieved 11 June 2021).
Simply Psychology

Merritt , Edwin T., Beaudin, James A., Cassidy, Charles

R. (2004). *Magnet and Specialized Schools of the Future -A Focus on Change,* R and L Education

Music "Flight of the Bumblebee" That Became Very Popular (2021). Galaxy Music Notes, https://galaxymusicnotes.com/pages/about-flight-of-the-bumblebee

Pepperman, Bob Taylor (2010). *Horace Mann's Troubling Legacy: The Education of Democratic Citizens (Americans Political Thought) University Press of Kansas: (1ˢᵗ Edition)*

"Platinum." *Merriam-Webster.com Dictionary*, Merriam-Webster (2021). https://www.merriam-webster.com/dictionary/platinum

Preble. Bill and Gordon, Rick (2014). *Transforming School Climate and Learning: Beyond Bullying and Compliance,* Corwin Press

Principles and Standards for School Mathematics (2000). National Council of Teachers of Mathematics

Professional Development (2013). The Glossary of Education Reform, https://www.edglossary.org/professional-development/

Rieall, Cindy and Boyles, Carolyn D. (2010). *Scaffolding Grade Level learning for Struggling Students,* Learning -Focused Solutions, Inc.

Smith, Margaret S. and Stein, Mary K. (2018). *5 Practices for Orchestrating Mathematical Discussions*, SAGE Publications

Smith, Rick and Dearborne, Grace (2016), *Conscious Classroom Management*, Conscious Teaching LLC; (2 nd edition)

Staker, Heather (2011). *The Rise of K-12 Blended Learning: Profiles of Emerging Models*, Innosight Institute

Stakeholder (2014). The Glossary of Education Reform, https://www.edglossary.org/stakeholder/

Swindali, Tommy (2020). *Music Production 2020: Everything You Need to Know About Producing Music, Studio Recording, Mixing, Mastering and Songwriting in 2020*, Fortune Publishing

The Constitution (2021). Interactive Constitution, https://constitutioncenter.org/interactive-constitution/the-constitution

What Every Teacher Should Know (2016). National Board for Professional Teaching Standards, https://www.nbpts.org/standards-five-core-propositions/

Whitburn, Joel (1992). *The Billboard Book of Top 40 Hits*, Billboard Books

Wong, Harry and Wong, Rebecca K. (2001) *The First Days of School: How to Be an Effective Teacher Wong*, Harry K Wong Publications

Index

G

H

I

M

N

O

P

S

About the Author: Dianne Reynolds

 Dianne Henry Reynolds served as an administrator for the Mobile County Public School System in Mobile, Alabama. She is a graduate of the University of South Alabama, where she received a Master's Degree in Administration and an Educational Specialist Degree. Much of her career has been dedicated to improvement efforts to help schools meet district and state accountability standards.

She has worked extensively with inner-city, rural, and magnet schools, gaining a unique perspective of the culture and climate of each. This diverse experience culminated in several personal and school honors, including National Board-Certified Teacher, National Blue Ribbon School, Terrel H. Bell Award for Outstanding Leadership, National Title I Distinguished School, and Alabama Torchbearer School, twice. She is a member of Alpha Kappa Alpha Sorority, Inc. and currently spends her time consulting and presenting at education conferences.

About the Author: Hattie Alexander

Hattie Alexander started her career as an educator in the Mobile Public School System. A graduate of Jackson State University with a BS degree in Elementary Education and Music receiving a masters in Guidance and Counseling and Certification in School Administration from Alabama State University.

Recently retiring after completing 40 years in education, Hattie has served as a teacher, counselor, and building principal for the past 26 years, serving as a leader of three different schools during her tenure with most assignments having to do with turning around schools. However, during the last 12 years, Hattie served as the principal of an IB Magnet school. Hattie Alexander led a team of educators receiving the following accolades: National Blue-Ribbon School, Lighthouse Blue Ribbon School, Alabama Banner School, Terrell Bell Awarded winner for leadership and Principal of the year for the County PTA association 2020. Additionally, Hattie is a proud member of Zeta Phi Beta

Sorority Inc. Hopefully, some experiences shared in *Platinum Principals: Making Your School a #1 Hit* will be useful to a novice administrator or teacher along the way.

Made in the USA
Coppell, TX
07 May 2022